MW01611019

Papal Supremacy and American Democracy

Papal Supremacy

The Roman Catholic Cornerstone and Stumblingblock

and

American Democracy

Its Religious Roots and Heritage

V. NORSKOV OLSEN

Loma Linda University Press
Loma Linda/Riverside, California

Copyright © 1987 by Loma Linda University Press
All rights reserved

No part of this publication may be reproduced, stored in a
retrieval system, or transmitted, in any form or by any means,
electronic, photocopying, recording, or otherwise, without the
prior written permission of the publisher.

Edited by Raymond F. Cottrell
Book design by V. Bailey Gillespie/Robert P. Dunn
Cover design by Joey Huerta
Electronic media by Schorschi Decker

Texts credited to N.E.B. are from the New English Bible © The Delegates
of the Oxford University Press and the Syndics of the Cambridge University
Press 1961, 1970. Reprinted by permission.

Texts marked R.S.V. are from the Revised Standard Version of the Bible,
copyrighted 1946, 1952 © 1971, 1973.

Cataloging in Publication Data
Olsen, V. Norskov (Viggo Norskov).
    Papal supremacy the Roman Catholic cornerstone and
stumblingblock and American democracy its religious roots and
heritage.
    Includes Bibliographical references.
1. Papacy. 2. Christianity and democracy—United States. 3.
Ecumenical movement. 4. Freedom of religion—History.
I. Title.
BX955.2   262.131

Library of Congress Catalog Card Number: 87-83037
ISBN 0-944450-01-6
Printed in the U.S.A. CP39860

Loma Linda University Press
Loma Linda, CA 92350
Riverside, CA 92515
10 9 8 7 6 5 4 3 2 1

Roman Catholicism as we know it is the product of twenty centuries of history. To understand it, we must try to understand this history. Not only is it the product of history but it involves a distinctive attitude toward history.

Jaroslav Pelikan

Give me liberty to know, to think, to believe, and to utter freely, according to conscience, above all liberties.

John Milton

Most Americans have been unaware of the fact that the moral dynamic of their democracy was the creation of one very specific Protestant ethical tradition.

James Hasting Nichols

CONTENTS

ACKNOWLEDGMENTS

The saying that "a man is himself plus the books he has read" is acknowledged by the biographical reference of the book. A considerable part of the historical material was brought together as a partial fulfillment of the requirement for a M.Th. degree. The writer is greatly indebted to his major professor the late Norman V. Hope, the Archibald Alexander Professor of church history Princeton Theological Seminary.

The help given so unstintingly by the Loma Linda University Library has been greatly appreciated. The computer facilities and the inter-library loan arrangements greatly facilitated my research.

I feel fortunate that Dr. Raymond Cottrell, a veteran editor, accepted the invitation by the University Press to be the book editor of my manuscript. Since he was one of the official journalists at the second Vatican Council, his insight and preface to the book hold special value. Dorene Sample, who assisted him in proofreading, also deserves thanks.

The unfailing support of Dr. Maurice Hodgen and Dr. Kenneth Vine, deans of the Graduate School and the School of Religion respectively, has meant much to the author.

The continual help of my secretary for many years, Antoinette Yakush, I do wish to acknowledge. On account of shortness of time she was ably assisted by Adriana Gneck.

Now that the book is ready for the press I wish to express my appreciation to the University Press Board chaired by Dr. Helen Ward Thompson, Vice President for Academic Affairs at Loma Linda University. Dr. V. Bailey Gillespie, the chief editor, with whom all the dealings for publication have taken place, deserves sincere gratitude for his cordiality and professional execution of the publication. The same must also be expressed regarding the University Press' associate editor, Dr. Robert P. Dunn.

Last but not least, my indebtedness to my wife remains beyond evaluation. Only by her unfailing support expressed in so many ways, was this book made possible.

V. Norskov Olsen—Loma Linda, California—1987

PREFACE

"We hold these truths to be self-evident, that all men are created equal, that they are endowed by their Creator with certain unalienable rights, that among these are Life, Liberty, and the pursuit of Happiness."

In these historic words dated July 4, 1776 the founding fathers of the United States of America set forth the fundamental principle on which the nation was founded and to which it still pledges allegiance. These unalienable rights are said to be self-evident by virtue of the fact that the Creator endowed all men with them; and what God has given, man has no right to take away. The Declaration of Independence thus based its concept of freedom, religious liberty, civil rights, justice, and democracy—of "government of the people, by the people, and for the people"—on the equality and dignity of all human beings, created in the image of God. Eleven years later the Federal Constitution, which begins with the words "We the people," expressed in concrete form the way in which these unalienable rights were to be made secure for all.

As the legend emblazoned on the great seal of the United States, *Novus ordo seclorum*—"A new order of the ages"—proclaims, full civil and religious liberty thus found tangible expression in government and society for the first time in history. Since then, through two centuries of drastically changing political and economic fortunes in the world, the relative stability, prosperity, and influence of the United States constitute an irrefutable endorsement of the principles on which it was founded. In the long run, this system works better than any other devised by man. As a role model of freedom, human rights, and opportunity the United States continues to attract, like a magnet, the people of many lands who aspire to make the most of their lives and their God-given faculties, and those of other lands who cherish these ideals look to the United States for leadership in defending them. The bicentennial celebrations of the Declaration of Independence in 1976 and of the Constitution in 1987 remind us that our heritage of freedom was not alone from the tyrannous rule of King George III, but from varying degrees of oppression in all past history elsewhere in the world as well.

Today we have become so accustomed to freedom that we are prone to take it for granted—as if, because it is "unalienable," we could never be deprived of it, or lose it even by default on our part. Our best protection against this false sense of security is to recall and keep untarnished in memory the long and arduous struggle over a period of centuries, in both Europe and the New World, as a result of which full civil and religious freedom became a reality, and to be aware (and to beware) of the vested interests and formidable forces that frustrated it. The fact that these vested interests live on today, more or less in hiding to be sure, reminds us that they could very well, in circumstances they find favorable, reassert themselves.

President Woodrow Wilson defined the goal of American entry into World War I as the ideal of making the world "safe for democracy"—of giving all people everywhere the opportunity to enjoy freedom. But two world wars have proved insufficient to attain that noble objective. Varying degrees of servitude and oppression are still the unhappy lot of a majority of the world's five billion people, even in some lands that pay lip service to civil and religious freedom. Freedom is not safe anywhere in the world, even in the United States, as long as oppression prevails anywhere in the world. The crusade of health care organizations to eliminate such scourges as smallpox and poliomyelitis from the face of the earth have been eminently more successful than those designed to eliminate injustice and oppression. So long as the desire to control other people or to take advantage of them for selfish reasons infects a few minds anywhere, the virus of tyranny remains endemic and could become epidemic. The fact that on five of the six continents authoritarian governments of one kind or another still control half or more of the human race, confronts the world with a potential threat to civil and religious freedom, a threat that is not imaginary or to be lightly dismissed. This book, however, is concerned primarily with more subtle forces, now slumbering, that pose a similar though less obvious threat. The ideal of complete separation between church and state, with a free church in a free state, is one that deserves to be kept ever in sharp focus, and tender loving care.

Those who do not learn from history are in imminent danger or repeating history. Such was Abraham Lincoln's meaning when he observed, on the eve of the Civil War between the States: "If we could first know where we are and whither we are tending, we could better judge what to do and how to do it." The basic issue before the nation in that bitter conflict could be seen in clear perspective only in terms of events and issues that transpired "fourscore and seven years ago" when the founding fathers "brought forth on this continent a new nation, conceived in liberty and dedicated to the proposition that all men are created equal." For Lincoln, the Civil War was a test of "whether that nation or any nation so conceived and so dedicated can long endure," and at Gettysburg he summoned his fellow Americans to "highly resolve that this nation under God shall have a new birth of freedom and that government of the people, by the people, for the people shall not perish from the earth."

Like Abraham Lincoln, the author of *Papal Supremacy and American Democracy* appeals to history for an understanding of the fundamental issues involved in preserving civil and religious liberty, and of latent forces which would, if they have an opportunity, deprive us of it. Like Abraham Lincoln with respect to the Civil War, he considers historical context essential to an accurate understanding of contemporary church-state issues. Like Abraham Lincoln, it is his purpose that we renew our resolve to preserve the fundamental principles for which this nation stands.

Upon first thought it may seem anomalous that a book whose focal concern in the separation of church and state and civil and religious liberty should bear the title *Papal Supremacy and American Democracy,* inasmuch as the two concepts are seemingly antithetical and somewhat mutually exclusive. But this very antithesis explains the anomaly. Prior to the Vatican II Declaration on Religious Freedom in 1965, papal theory and practice had always, without exception, been adamantly opposed to civil and religious liberty, democracy, and the separation of church and state. The papal Syllabus of Errors of 1864 affirmed this antithesis for modern times by explicitly condemning all of these principles, together with the idea that anyone had the right to worship according to his conscience instead of as the church might direct. It anathematized anyone who claimed

> That every man is free to embrace and profess the religion he shall believe to be true, guided by the light of reason (§3).

> That the Church ought to be separated from the State, and the State from the Church (§6).

> That the Church has not the power of availing herself of forces, or of any direct or indirect temporal power (§5).

"Error" 39 similarly condemned the idea that "the commonwealth is the origin and source of all rights"—the democratic principle that government is "of the people, by the people, for the people."

Although the Syllabus of Errors has never been withdrawn or renounced, some may aver that promulgation of the Declaration on Religious Liberty by the second Vatican Council tacitly renders it obsolete. That was probably the intention of most if not all of the American bishops at the council, who were unquestionably sincere in their persistent endeavor to secure its passage. The phenomenal success and strength of the Catholic Church in America had persuaded the American members of the hierarchy that full religious liberty is good for the church. For example, weekly attendance at mass in the United States approximates forty of fifty per cent of the entire membership, compared with an average of about three per cent in Roman Catholic countries of Europe and Latin America where concordats assure the church favored status and often financial support.

A declaration on religious liberty was not on the original agenda of the council, and as originally framed by Father John Courtney Murray, an American Jesuit scholar, it clearly affirmed the concept of genuine religious freedom in tones that would meet the approval of its most ardent Protestant advocates. A majority of the Vatican II bishops, however, could not be persuaded to accept the document in its original form, and only the later inclusion of provisos protecting the favored status of the church, by concordats, was it possible to win their more or less reluctant approval. On their part, the American bishops considered the statement essential, not only on the basis of principle but also for the credibility of the church in the United States. The only consideration that made such a declaration acceptable—to most but not all of the bishops—was the fact that the Roman Catholic Church itself was in dire need of religious liberty in Communist countries.

Rejection of the original religious liberty schema with its complete separation of church and state, by the council majority, and eventual approval with provision for church-state collaboration and favored status for the Catholic Church wherever possible, by nine-tenths of the bishops, reflects a significant difference of opinion on the subject among the members of the ruling hierarchy. The fact that the majority objected to full religious liberty as provided by the original schema, and that 224 (or ten per cent) of the bishops voted against it even in its modified form, reflects overwhelming opposition within the hierarchy to the concept of full religious freedom.

This suggests that the Declaration on Religious Freedom reflects a de facto concession to the modern mood rather than a basic revision of the historical position of the church. It is certain that members of the roman curia at the Vatican have not, like the American bishops, become ardent advocates of full religious freedom. Dogmatically and ideologically, its claim to exclusive possession of the keys to heaven, to the authority of the church over the State, and to favored status and government support has not changed.

It must not be forgotten that, as history amply demonstrates, civil rights do not flourish in lands where the people do not enjoy religious liberty, and that freedom on the part of a church to administer its own affairs without interference on the part of civil authority does not exist when the church is in any way dependent on public support.

Such is the *raison d' etre* of *Papal Supremacy and American Democracy*. This book is motivated by concern for the preservation of full civil and religious liberty and the effective separation of church and state promised in the Declaration of Independence and guaranteed by the First Amendment to the Constitution, and by the centuries of struggle between an authoritarian church and courageous individuals who dedicated their lives and fortunes to the quest for translating this ideal into reality. The facts of history set forth, together with the unaltered dogma and ideology of the church, portend the possible revival of intolerance and the loss of full civil and religious liberty in some future time of crisis.

With a personal perspective formed by the golden rule and the Sermon on the Mount, the author approaches his subject, not with the incendiary fervor of a crusader, but with the calm detachment appropriate for the scholar that he is. He writes with malice toward none and charity for all, not in the Catholic-baiting mood that was popular among certain Protestants prior to Vatican Council II. He deals with the facts of history objectively, in a way that will merit the approval of any informed Catholic scholar. As a matter of fact, not a few Catholic scholars such as Hans Küng have written much more disapprovingly about papal supremacy and infallibility than Dr. Olsen does. The author cites both Catholic and Protestant writers nearly four hundred times in less than two hundred pages, meticulously documenting each point beyond the possibility of quibble or doubt. This thorough documentation makes *Papal Supremacy and American Democracy* a rich source of historical information on the subject to which many in years to come will refer as an authority in its own right. This book is not a polemic against the Catholic Church, which the title may suggest to some, but one that will earn the confidence and respect of informed Catholics and Protestants alike who value the principles of civil and religious freedom. Only a person with intimate knowledge and mature understanding of the subject could bring together, as Dr. V. Norskov Olsen does, such a wealth of relevant historical information in so compact and readable form, with the evident scholarship and skill this book reflects.

Raymond F. Cottrell—Loma Linda, California—1987

1

PAPAL SUPREMACY, JURISDICTION, AND INFALLIBILITY:
Its Beginnings and Development

The Roman Catholic Church is an institution unique in the history of the Christian era. For centuries its teaching and practices have exerted an influence not only on purely religious matters, but also on the secular life of that part of the world which is called Christian. "Roman Catholicism as we know it is the product of twenty centuries of history. To understand it, we must try to understand this history. Not only is it the product of history, but it involves a distinctive attitude toward history."[1] Thus writes Jaroslav Pelikan in his well-known book, *The Riddle of Roman Catholicism.* To his observation we will add the words of Jean Guitten, "It is characteristic of the Catholic Church to change, but always staying the same and even more so. The Catholic Church changes in order to stay herself."[2]

Interwoven with the history of Roman Catholicism is the story of the pope: his supremacy, jurisdiction, and infallibility. It may even be said that in the history of the latter we find the influential cause of much of the history of the Roman Catholic Church in general. We will first observe the beginnings and the development of the papal claim to universal supremacy and infallibility. The Vatican Council I of 1870 was the climactic event of that story.

VATICAN COUNCIL I

Viva Pio Nono Papa infallible! These words echoed and re-echoed in the basilica of St. Peter in Rome on the eventful July 18, 1870 when the great crowd, having heard the message of papal infallibility, jubilantly expressed their applause. "In the midst of one of the fiercest storms ever known to break across the city, accompanied by thunder and lightning, while rain poured in through the broken glass of the roof close to the spot where the Pope was standing, Pius IX. read in the darkness, by the aid of a candle, the momentous affirmation of his own Infallibility."[3]

The fierce storm and dense darkness, the thunder and lightening that accompanied the reading of this document, caused adherents of the papacy to compare the event to the lawgiving at Mount Sinai; on the other hand, opponents saw in the wrath of the elements a sign of God's anger. By both friend and critic the declaration of papal absolutism was considered to be the most momentous event in the long history of the papacy.

On that day the document entitled *Dogmatic Constitution on the Catholic Faith* was decreed. It contains three fundamental concepts which were made into dogma: the supremacy, the universal jurisdiction, and the infallibility of the pope.

Each of the four chapters of this document closes with an anathema, which gives a clear indication of the far-reaching consequence of the papal claims. First is mentioned "the Institution of the Apostolic Primacy in blessed Peter," and then it is declared: "If any one, therefore, shall say that blessed Peter the Apostle was not appointed the Prince of all the Apostles and the visible Head of the whole Church Militant; or that the same directly and immediately received from the same our Lord Jesus Christ a primacy of honor only, and not of true and proper jurisdiction; let him be anathema."

In chapter two "the Perpetuity of the Primacy of blessed Peter in the Roman Pontiffs" is taught, and the chapter concludes by saying: "If, then, any should deny that it is by the institution of Christ the Lord, or by divine right, that blessed Peter should have a perpetual line of successors in the Primacy over the universal Church, or that the Roman Pontiff is the successor of blessed Peter in this primacy: let him be anathema."

A third anathema is expressed at the close of the discussion of the "Power and Nature of the Primacy of the Roman Pontiff." This part of the document emphasizes that the pontifical office is not "merely of inspection or direction" but "of full and supreme power of jurisdiction over the universal Church, not only in things which belong to faith and morals, but also in those which relate to the discipline and government of the Church spread throughout the world."

The pope possesses not merely the principal part but the fullness of the supreme power of jurisdiction.   Further, it is "ordinary [supreme] and immediate, both over each and all the churches, and over each and all the pastors and the faithful."4 A person who denies this should be anathematized.

Pius IX (1846-1878) was the pope who had summoned, directed, and controlled Vatican I. More than anyone and anything else he was the initiator and promoter of the dogma of infallibility. When he decreed the immaculate conception of the Virgin Mary (Dec. 8, 1854) he had already exercised the infallibility doctrine. He asserts that "if some should presume to think in their hearts otherwise than we have defined (which God forbid)," then "they shall know and thoroughly understand that they are by their own judgment condemned, have made shipwreck concerning the faith, and fallen away from the unity of the Church."5

In the course of our study we will return to Vatican I in several connections. At present we will merely notice the formulation of the dogma of infallibility and cite the conclusion in total.

> We teach and define that it is a dogma divinely revealed: that the Roman Pontiff, when he speaks *ex cathedra*, that is, when in discharge of the office of pastor and doctor of all Christians, by virtue of his supreme Apostolic authority, he defines a doctrine regarding faith or morals to be held by the universal Church, by the divine assistance promised to him in blessed Peter, is possessed of that infallibility with which the divine Redeemer willed that his Church should be endowed for defining doctrine regarding faith or morals; and that therefore such definitions of the Roman Pontiff are irreformable of themselves,

and not from the consent of the Church. But if any one—which may God avert—presume to contradict this our definition: let him be anathema.6

The three concepts: papal supremacy, universal jurisdiction and infallibility, defined and proclaimed as dogma by Vatican Council I, have often been considered as discrete concepts but, as we shall see, there is an inner connection between them; the third follows as a corollary of the first two, which may be considered twin concepts.

Acceptance of the dogma of papal infallibility by the Vatican Council I was a unique event in the history of Christendom with weighty consequences, the result of which we have not yet seen. How the claim of infallibility came about and how to perceive it, can only be answered in the light of history.

THE CHURCH OF ROME:
Its Founding and Early History

According to "authoritative" Roman Catholic tradition there is considerable evidence that Peter remained in Rome as its first bishop and died there a martyr in A.D. 67. The New Testament, however, is silent on the matter, and its indirect evidence suggests the opposite. The first dozen chapters of the Acts of the Apostles make no reference to Peter being in Rome, and the book closes with reference to Paul's sojourn in Rome, but nothing about Peter. Paul's epistle to the Romans (A.D. 57 or 58) makes no reference to Peter. During Paul's two-year imprisonment in Rome in the early sixties he wrote four letters, none of which mention Peter. We find that Paul rebuked Peter at Antioch (Gal. 2:11-14). Peter's statement in 1 Peter 5:13, "She who is at Babylon, who is likewise chosen, sends you greetings," has been used to indicate that Peter was in Rome by explaining that Babylon is a cryptic name for Rome. This explanation is not conclusive and other interpretations are equally plausible.

How Christianity originated in Rome we do not know. Luke tells us that in the audience gathered on the day of Pentecost were "visitors from Rome, both Jews and proselytes" (Acts 2:10).

Some of these may have accepted the gospel and on their return brought it to Rome. Suggestions have also been made to the effect that the church was founded by Christians from Antioch.7 The one sure thing we do know is that when Paul wrote his letter to the Romans (A.D. 58), he could say, "Your faith is proclaimed in all the world" (Rom. 1:8). Several Christian writings produced in the post-apostolic era (c. A.D. 100-150) conspicuously make no reference to the founding of the church in Rome by Peter or his subsequent martyrdom there. Justin Martyr, an early Christian apologist, lived in Rome in the middle of the second century where he directed a Christian school. Oscar Cullman comments: "Neither in his Apologies nor in the Dialogue with Trypho is Peter's Roman residence mentioned. This is the more striking in view of the fact that he speaks three times of Simon the magician, who in this period was regarded as the great opponent of Peter."8

Those who advocate Peter's stay in Rome cite two early Christian writers, Clement of Rome (c. A.D. 95) and Ignatius of Antioch (A.D. 107). At best their statements convey mere probabilities and are inconclusive. When Paul wrote his epistle to the Romans (A.D. 58) he could say, "Your faith is proclaimed in all the world" (Romans 1:8). This is only natural for a church in the capital city of the empire, and at the close of the century the letter of Clement to the church of Corinth substantiates the same, as also docs Ignatius. Regarding the letter of Clement, H. Burn-Murdoch writes: "The later Roman Theory supposes that the Church of Rome derives all its authority from the bishop of Rome as the successor of St. Peter. History inverts this relation and shows that, as a matter of fact, the power of the bishop of Rome was built upon the power of the Church of Rome. It was originally a primacy, not of the episcopate, but of the church."9

Ignatius of Antioch, on his way to Rome as a prisoner, wrote seven letters, one of which was for the church in Rome. In it Ignatius writes: "I do not command you, as Peter and Paul did."10 Bishop W. S. Kerr gives this explanation: "This only means that he does not assume apostolic authority to command. It is a favourite form of speech with him. To the Ephesians he says: 'I do not give you orders as being somewhat' or 'some one important'. To the

Trallians: 'I did not consider myself qualified to give you orders as an apostle, being a convict.'"11

The first clear reference to Peter being in Rome comes from the close of the second century. Dionysius, leader of the church in Corinth (A.D. 168-177) wrote to the people in Rome: "By so great an admonition you bound together the foundations of the Romans and the Corinthians by Peter and Paul, for both of them taught together in our Corinth and were our founders, and together also taught in Italy the same place and were martyred at the same time."12 The quotation is given by Eusebius, church historian at the time of Constantine in the fourth century. One historical error is obvious; namely, that Peter and Paul together founded the Church in Corinth. In light of 1 Corinthians 3:6 and 4:15, this is impossible. Paul writes: "I planted, Apollos watered, but God was causing the growth" and "In Christ Jesus I became your father through the gospel." If Dionysius is wrong in one instance he could also be wrong in the other. However, from this time onward references to Peter being in Rome become general.

In his treatise *Against Heresies,* (about A.D. 185) Irenaeus stressed that the gospel which the Apostles proclaimed had been "handed down to us in the Scriptures, to be the ground and pillar of our faith." In this connection he mentions that "Peter and Paul were preaching at Rome, and laying the Foundations of the Church." Later he repeats the same when he mentions "the very great, the very ancient, and universally known Church founded and organized at Rome by the two most glorious apostles, Peter and Paul."13

In each of these statements, Peter is not the sole founder, but is mentioned together with Paul. In the light of early historical evidence, it would not be correct to speak of the church of Rome as the See of Peter or to say that the popes occupy the chair of St. Peter. However, in order to fulfill what Roman Catholics believe to be authentic, each pope to the present time is always the bishop of Rome.

When we trace the beginnings and further development of the preeminence of the church in Rome and its bishops we will notice, as our study progresses, that it was not Apostolic origins but the geographical and political location of Rome which enhanced the church. The church in Jerusalem, the mother church of Christianity, sank into insignificance after the destruction of Jerusalem and the temple, A.D. 70, and the church founded abroad counted far more.

The political and intellectual greatness of Rome as the capital of a vast empire was an advantage to the Christian church established there. The early church councils accounted for the rank of the church in Rome by its location. The Council of Chalcedon in A.D. 451 gave as the reason for Rome's primacy the fact that it was the imperial city, not that it was the See of Peter. "For to the throne of Old Rome, the Fathers gave privileges with good reason, because it was the imperial city."14

The church in Rome developed very early a consciousness of strength, as illustrated by the Paschal controversy of the second century. The Christians of Asia Minor followed the Jewish calendar for the time to celebrate the Christian Passover. Thus it was held on the fourteenth of Nisan, and that could be any day of the week. On the contrary the church in Rome always celebrated on the first Sunday after the full moon in the month of March.

Between A.D. 150 and 155 the question regarding the correct time to celebrate Easter came into discussion in connection with a visit by Polycarp, bishop of Smyrna, to Anicetus, bishop of Rome. Polycarp and Anicetus discussed the matter but could not reach any agreement. They communed with each other and parted in peace.15

Victor, who became bishop of Rome in A.D. 190, manifested a very different attitude. He was determined to secure uniformity. Accordingly, he excommunicated Polycrates who led the bishops of Asia Minor in opposition to Rome in changing the date for Easter. This action met with protest, notably from Irenaeus, who admonished Victor "that he should not cut off whole churches of God which observed the tradition of an ancient custom."16 However, it indicates the growing authority which the bishop of Rome usurped at the close of the second century.

In the second century Christianity was challenged by a form of Christianity and pagan philosophy named Gnosticism. As a threefold defense against Gnosticism in the second century the Christian church developed the New Testament canon, the concept that truth was preserved in apostolic succession, and creedal statements of faith. In this struggle against Gnosticism the Roman church was the champion of orthodoxy. Marcion, a Christian gnostic, came to Rome about A.D. 140 but was excluded from the church. At this time, Justin Martyr was the church's apologist and wrote successfully against heretics, but as already noticed he does not make reference to the Apostle Peter.

The development of the monarchical episcopate by which a local church was governed by a single bishop instead of a group of presbyters, emerged in the second century, and the statements by Dionysius, Irenaeus, and Tertullian regarding Peter and Paul must be seen in the light of this development. J. N. D. Kelly writes: "In the late 2nd or early 3rd century the tradition identified Peter as the first bishop of Rome. This was a natural development once the monarchical episcopate...emerged in Rome in the mid-2nd century."[17]

The function of the monarchical episcopate in Rome and elsewhere was obvious in the Paschal controversy, but can also be illustrated by the governance of the church at the time of the Decian persecution in the middle of the third century. For this subject, we will turn to Cyprian, who was elected bishop of Carthage (A.D. 249), a stronghold of Christianity in North Africa. It is to Cyprian that we owe the early but classical definition of the monarchical episcopate: "Ye ought to know that the bishop is in the church and this church in the bishop; and if anyone be not with the bishop, that he is not in the church." Contrary to the later Roman Catholic concept but in harmony with the Orthodox and Anglican churches' view, Cyprian asserts: "The episcopate is one, each part of which is held by each one in its entirety."[18]

A further enhancement of the right of jurisdiction by the bishop of Rome is found in the early years of the christological controversy, also during the third century. Those opposed to the orthodox christology were called Monarchians. The Monarchians fell into two very unlike classes, those who held that Jesus was the Son of God by adoption—the so-called Dynamic Monarchians—and those who held that Christ was but a temporary manifestation in flesh of the one, everlasting spirit of God, without permanent individuation, distinct from the Father. This party was known as Modalistic Monarchians. Paul of Samosata was a representative of the first group, and Sabellius of the second group, whose teaching is known as Sabellianism. During the struggle Rome and the West reached conclusions regarding the nature of Christ that antedate the decision of the Council of Nicea in A.D. 325. At this time both Rome (A.D. 259-269) and Alexandria (A.D. 249-265) had bishops by the name of Dionysius. Dionysius of Alexandria combatted the widespread Eastern Sabellianism, but what he wrote seemed open to criticism, as if it leaned towards the opposite heresy. Thereupon Dionysius of Rome issued a summary of the christological problem in which he gave direction to the bishop of Alexandria. In the fourth and fifth centuries Rome refers to the correspondence between the two bishops in order to claim her prerogatives over Alexandria.

The Dynamic Monarchians were strongly represented in Antioch, whose bishop (A.D. 260-270) was Paul of Samosata. Several synods met to consider his position, but inasmuch as Zenobia, the queen of Palmyra, trusted him, no sentence could be carried out against him. But when Emperor Aurelian defeated her he banished Paul from his chair. During the discussion about disposing of the church property in Antioch, Emperor Aurelian made the important decision that it be given to those whom the bishops of Italy and Rome should appoint. Church historian Eusebius commented on the emperor's banishment of Paul: "Thus this man was driven out of the church, with extreme disgrace, by the worldly power."[19] This exercise of the civil power and assignment of the property in Antioch to the bishop of Rome had far reaching consequences in Rome's pursuit for supremacy that would be repeated often in years to come.

The third century thus set the stage for the bishop of Rome's claim to universal supremacy and jurisdiction. As already noted and to be still further confirmed, the stage was not primarily set by the theological concept of Rome as the See of Peter, even though this argument was used, but by the political situation—as A.B. Hasler points out: "As a matter of fact, however, it was not Apostolic origins but political position that determined who got authority in the Church."[20]

The establishment of Constantine's state-church made the church "Roman" in a non-theological, non-ecclesiological sense. During the Middle Ages the papacy sought to realize the Roman ideal of one people, one religion, one language, and one supreme ruler, who was a representative of the divine. The Roman judicial system and governmental structure were taken over into the organization and governance of the church. Pagan Rome literally grew into Papal Rome. The situation has been summarized in these words:

> The reconciliation of the Roman Empire with Christianity under Constantine the Great (ca. 280-337) and the establishment of Christianity as the state religion altered the nature of churchly offices. A church hierarchy grew up that corresponded to the state's. Church officials received numerous privileges, some of them rising to the rank of senators. Civil and religious laws were now often identical. Canon law entered upon a boom period. After the partial breakdown of the Roman Empire, high church officials also took over political functions.21

Having referred to the fact that "it was the emperor who had the greatest interest in settling doctrinal disputes" and who "convoked ecumenical councils and largely dictated their results," Hasler closes with the observation: "But as yet no one said anything about infallibility. If anybody was infallible it was the emperor."22 We will examine the subject of church-state relations in other connections, but in the meantime note that when this topic is evaluated in the light of history three different concepts surface:

1. Roman Catholicism sees a divinely guided historical development of the Roman Catholic Church, from Peter down through the centuries.

2. The so-called magisterial reformers of the sixteenth century (who allied themselves with the state) perceived the Constantinian state-church as the beginning of a glorious period for the church. They valued the ancient church councils, generally summoned by the emperor. In their opinion, however, as the bishop of Rome took over the vacated prerogatives of the emperor and papal supremacy developed, the church became more and more "Roman" and ceased to be apostolic and holy.

3. Those branches of the Protestant Reformation who considered the Lutheran and Anglican church-state relation as evil, perceived the establishment of Constantine's state-church the first great apostasy in the history of Christendom. Accordingly they sought, not merely a reformation of the church, but the restitution of the apostolic or primitive church of the New Testament. The difference between an episcopalian and presbyterian form of church organization was also vital to them, inasmuch as they believed the latter to be true. In the following historical survey it will be helpful to keep these three evaluations in mind.

MEDIEVAL POPES CLAIM
UNIVERSAL JURISDICTION

The concept of equality of authority among the bishops remained prominent until the time of Constantine and after, except that the bishops of provincial capital cities became first in rank. According to canon nine of the Council of Antioch (A.D. 341): "The bishops of every province must be aware that the bishop presiding in the metropolis (the civil capital) has charge of the whole province; because all who have business come together from all quarters to the metropolis. For this reason it is decided that he should also hold the foremost rank."[23]

This canon increased the power of the metropolitan bishop. As yet, however, the bishop of Rome had authority only in his own province, as the others had in theirs. Furthermore, the reason given for the first rank of the metropolitan bishops was the significance of the city in the life of the province. The same principle applied to Rome as the capital city of the empire, and later to Constantinople in the East. This is illustrated in the pontificate of Innocent I (A.D. 402-417) who found his own province confining and sought jurisdiction over his fellow bishops in the other provinces as his reply to letters from the Council of Carthage (A.D. 416) indicates: "For you decided that it was proper to refer to our judgment, knowing what is due to the Apostolic See, since all we who are set in this place, desire to follow the Apostle from whom the very episcopate and whole authority of this name is derived."[24] He further specifies "that nothing be brought to finality, even in distant and remote provinces, unless it come to the knowledge of this see, so that by its authority the whole just pronouncement may be confirmed: and that from thence—like as all waters issue from their natal fount, and the pure streams of an incorrupt head flow thorough diverse regions of the whole world."[25]

When Alaric sacked Rome in A.D. 410, Pope Innocent was virtually governor of the city. He exhorted Alaric to spare the churches. When the Romans tried to negotiate a peace between Alaric and Emperor Honorius, Innocent went to Ravenna when their deputation did not succeed. To a large degree Innocent prepared the way for Pope Leo the Great (A.D. 440-461).

In the person of Pope Leo the idea of the papacy became reality. He has been called "the Father of the Papacy."[26] Immediately upon assuming the episcopacy he began to assert the authority of his See by formulating the Petrine theory. In an early sermon he speaks of Peter always being recognized in Peter's See.[27]

Peter "was ordained before the rest in such a way that from his being called the Rock, from his being pronounced the Foundation, from his being constituted the Doorkeeper of the kingdom of heaven, from his being set as the Umpire to bind and to loose, whose judgments shall retain their validity in heaven, from all these mystical titles we might know the nature of his association with Christ." This work of Peter is still carried on by his successor. Leo I could therefore say: "And so if anything is rightly done and rightly decreed by us, if anything is won from the mercy of God by our daily supplications, it is of his work and merits whose power lives and whose authority prevails in his See." In other words, in each pope Peter as the chief apostle is "reincarnated." The sermon was given on the anniversary of his elevation to the pontificate and he points out that the occasion was in the honor of St. Peter for "in my humble person he may be recognized and honoured." Leo could therefore say: "When therefore we utter our exhortations in your ears, holy brethren, believe that he is speaking whose representative we are: because it is his warning that we give, nothing else but his teaching that we preach."[28]

In another sermon Leo I follows the tradition by saying that the church of Rome was founded by Peter and Paul and made the citadel of the world. Said Leo: "These are they who promoted thee to such glory, that being made a holy nation, a chosen people, a priestly and royal state, and the head of the world through the blessed Peter's holy See thou didst obtain a wider sway by the worship of God than by earthly government."[29]

The Council of Chalcedon (A.D. 451) was summoned for the purpose of settling the discussion on the true nature of Christ. Pope Leo was not present at the council, but had written the so-called Tome, in which he sets forth the view which the West had entertained since the third century. It was read at the council and accepted by acclamation: "Peter has spoken by Leo." However, as will be noticed in another connection, Pope Leo's claim of supremacy and universal jurisdiction was denied in canons enacted at the council.

Gregory the Great (A.D. 590-604), "last of the Latin fathers and the first of the popes, connects the ancient with the mediaeval church."[30] He contended strongly for the supremacy of Rome and exercised constant supervision over bishops in all parts of the East and the West. The spiritual and temporal authority he exercised gave birth and form to the papacy of the Middle Ages. In addition to "his multitudinous duties, he was virtual king of Italy." Not only head, he was also "the first Pope to become in act and in influence, if not in name, the temporal sovereign of the West."[31]

Nicholas I (A.D. 858-867), third of the three popes styled "The Great" and the only outstanding pope between Gregory I and Gregory VII (1073-1085), made full use of the political situation arisen from the division of the empire of Charlemagne. Modern France and Germany have their beginning in this division, which weakened the power of the secular rulers as compared with the papacy.

To the emperor in the East and the patriarch of Constantinople, Nicholas I wrote several letters in connection with the election of a new patriarch after the former had been deposed by the emperor. In these letters the pope expresses papal supremacy and jurisdiction in the most clear language. He affirms "that no decision must be given on any new matter that arises without the consent of the Roman See and the Roman Pontiff." It is as vicar of Peter that the pope can exercise full authority. He wrote: "After him, his vicars, sincere servers of God, free from the mists which are wont to cause men to wander from the right path, have received the same privilege, and have steadily persevered in the government of the Lord's sheep which has been entrusted to them."32 Addressing the emperor he further reinforces his authority by stating: "These privileges, by the words of Christ, founded on Blessed Peter, ever reverenced in the Church, cannot be lessened or changed; for human efforts cannot move the foundation which God has laid.... The privileges of this See existed before your empire, they will remain after you, and they will remain inviolate as long as Christianity shall be preached."33

While the supremacy, thus expressed by Nicholas, failed in the case just mentioned, it then achieved the desired result in the case of Lothaire II, the king of Lorraine, who had divorced his wife and married his mistress. Theutberga, the wife of Lothaire and also daughter of the count of Burgundy, appealed to the pope. The archbishops of Trier and Cologne had supported Lothaire. The Pope declared void their sanction to the divorce, excommunicated them and compelled the king to take back his wife. No wonder that Hincmar, archbishop of Rheims, complained that "Nicholas, who is called the Pope... makes himself the emperor of the whole world."34

Opposition to the claim of universal jurisdiction by the bishop of Rome was always present, but as the clamor became more insistent, as with Nicholas I, animosity intensified, especially in the East.

The Eastern Church recognized four patriarchates with equal rights—Constantinople, Alexandria, Antioch, and Jerusalem. As the estrangement between Rome and the East grew to hostility a separation was inevitable. The final separation (1054) came when Pope Leo IX (1049-1054), and Cerularius, patriarch of Constantinople (1043-1059), anathematized and excommunicated each other. The schism, dividing Christian East and West, is still a silent protest against the universal jurisdiction of the pope and a continuing stumbling block between the Eastern Orthodox churches and the church of Rome.

Between 1073 and 1302 the papacy made its most lofty claims to universal supremacy and also attained its maximum power. Gregory VII (1073-1085) summed up his conception of the pope in a document entitled *Dictatus Papae*. This document makes the pope God's representative on earth, with absolute power over the church and secular rulers:

> That the Roman church was founded by God alone.
> That the Roman pontiff alone can with right be called universal.
> That he alone can depose or reinstate bishops....
> That he alone may use the imperial insignia....
> That it may be permitted to him to depose emperors....
> That a sentence passed by him may be retracted by no one; and that he himself, alone of all, may retract it.
> That he himself may be judged by no one....
> That the Roman church has never erred; nor will it err to all eternity, the Scripture bearing witness....
> That he who is not in peace with the Roman church shall not be considered catholic....
> That he may absolve subjects from their fealty to wicked men.[35]

To a large degree Gregory VII succeeded in realizing the lofty ideals of the *Dictatus Papae*. "Gregory VII, Innocent III and Boniface VIII stand out as the three popes who stated most clearly the claims of the papacy both in spiritual matters and secular: but Innocent III alone made good the claim."[36] On various occasions in the history of the church we find the title "Vicar of Christ" used with reference to the bishops, but Innocent III claimed the title exclusively for himself, as holder of the unique chair of St. Peter.[37] In a letter to the patriarch of Constantinople in 1199 he stated: "The pope is the vicar of Christ, yea of God himself. Not only is he intrusted with the Dominion of the Church, but also with the rule of the whole world. Like Melchizedek, he is at once king and priest.... So are they also his vicar."[38]

Before the time of Innocent III the popes had called themselves vicars of Peter, but since then their title has been "Vicar of Christ." In his Unam Sanctam Pope Boniface declared: "There is one body of the one and only church, and one head, not two heads, as if the church were a monster. And this head is Christ and his vicar, Peter and his successor."39

The next significant pontificate was that of Boniface VIII (1294-1303). His bull, *Unam Sanctam,* expressed the proudest, most ambitious and highest claim regarding the universality of papal power and jurisdiction:

> By the words of the gospel we are taught that the two swords, namely, the spiritual authority [sic] and temporal are in the power of the church.... Both swords, therefore, the spiritual and the temporal, are in the power of the Church. The former is to be used by the church, the latter for the church; the one by the hand of the priest, the other by the hand of kings and knights, but at the command and permission of the priest.... And we must necessarily admit that the spiritual power surpasses any earthly power in dignity and honor, because spiritual things surpass temporal things.... Therefore if the temporal power errs, it will be judged by the spiritual power, and if the lower spiritual power errs, it will be judged by its superior. But if the highest spiritual power errs, it cannot be judged by men, but by God alone.... We therefore declare, say, and affirm that submission on the part of every man to the bishop of Rome is altogether necessary for his salvation.40

Climaxing the expression of more than a thousand years of persistent, though unjustified, claims for universal supremacy, Boniface VIII placed the capstone on the medieval papal structure of supremacy and universal jurisdiction. There is a direct relationship between Unam Sanctam and the declaration of papal infallibility at Vatican I, for which it laid the foundation.

The question may now be asked: Why did it take nearly six centuries, from 1302 to 1870, before Unam Sanctam became the first *Dogmatic Constitution on the Church of Christ,* or the doctrine of universal supremacy became the doctrine of papal infallibility? The answer is a story of "civil war" and "revolution" inside the church caused by opposition to, and defense of, the dogma of papal authority.

Boniface had expressed the proudest and highest claims of papal supremacy, but his excommunications and threats of deposition went unheeded. A conspiracy was formed against him and he was seized at Anagni, where he had taken refuge. Yet he was rescued and taken to Rome, where he died a month later. He had been as one just about to place the crowning tower on a great edifice, only to find the walls of the vast structure crashing beneath him. The following observation should be noted:

> In the humiliation of Boniface VIII., the state gained a signal triumph over the papacy....Two hundred years after the conflict between Boniface and Philip the Fair, Luther was to fight the battle for the spiritual sovereignty of the individual man. These two principles, set aside by the priestly pride and theological misunderstanding of the Middle Ages, belong to the foundation of modern civilization.[41]

The pontificate of Boniface VIII marks the highest claim to papal supremacy, but also the beginning of a process of reaction against the universal jurisdiction of the pope.

2

ROME'S INTERNAL CONFLICT

The tragic history of the papacy after the pontificate of Boniface VIII testifies to the fact that the papal claim for universal supremacy became its Achilles' heel. During the short periods when the papal ideal seemed to triumph and the popes actually exercised universal supremacy, they always committed the future to a policy that seemed destined to sweep away the papacy altogether. The mingling of temporal and spiritual supremacy inevitably prejudiced the pope's spiritual authority, generally speaking, because as temporal rulers they did not give evidence of being superior to secular rulers.

THE POPE IN EXILE. THE PAPAL SCHISM

The collapse of papal supremacy with the pontificate of Boniface VIII soon became apparent. In 1305 the archbishop of Bordeaux was elected pope and took the name Clement V. He never crossed the Alps into Italy, and in 1309 he moved the papal court from Rome to Avignon, a city along the river Rhone in France, where the papal court remained until 1377. This period has been called the Babylonian Captivity of the papacy because it nearly equalled in length the seventy years of exile of the Jews in Babylon. During this period there were seven popes, all French.

In 1378 began the papal schism which lasted until 1417. During these years there were two series of popes, one at Rome and the other at Avignon, each duly elected and with a set of cardinals, and both under reciprocal excommunication. One part of Europe adhered to Rome, the other to Avignon. In 1409 cardinals from the two papal courts met at the Council of Pisa to elect a new pope instead of the two rival popes. The new pope, who took the name Alexander V, set up court at Bologna. Neither of the two other popes would resign, thus there were now three duly elected popes, each with his own papal court and cardinals.

The nations of Europe divided their allegiance among the three papal courts, where each of the rival popes was proclaiming eternal condemnation over his rivals. The whole of Christendom was really under ban, since each of the popes excommunicated the other two and their followers. This situation lasted until the Council of Constance, 1414-1418. The Babylonian Captivity and the Great Schism made null the ideal of a living infallible guide or the doctrine of the incarnated Peter in each pope.

The papal apologists and opponents of the time can be divided into four groups. The first group were "those who stood forth as champions of the sweeping claims of the medieval Pope as a general proposition, but who were personally hostile to Boniface VIII." The second group included "those unqualified supporters of Boniface VIII in his adherence to the position taken by Gregory VII and Innocent III and also in his course of action." The third was "the oligarchical party, who sought to change Papal constitution by placing sovereign power in the college of cardinals." The fourth was "the conciliar-episcopal party, who defended the supremacy of a general council over the Pope and sought to increase the prerogatives and powers of the bishops." Of these four Alexander C. Flick says: "A study of the arguments advanced by these four parties shows that they may be reduced to two general factions, namely, the supporters of the Papal theory, and the opponents of the fundamental Papal claims, who sought to locate the sovereignty of the Church in some other ecclesiastical body and not in the state."[1]

As will be noted, the "civil war" fought at Vatican Council I was a decisive battle in a larger "war" that had been going on for several centuries between the papalist party and the conciliarists. The latter sought to transform the papacy from an absolute monarchy into a constitutional monarchy or system in which power was not seated in one person but in a group of men, as for example, the bishops and cardinals. For the conciliarists the highest authority would then be a general council composed of delegates duly elected and rightly representative of all Christendom. The whole work of the conciliar movement with its religious, political, and social consequences is the most important aspect of ecclesiastical history in the fifteenth century.

THE REFORMING COUNCILS

The idea of a general council as the best means of bringing an end to the papal schism won more and more favor. A council that met in Pisa in 1409 to replace the two popes failed, and as a result there were now three popes. This council, however, was unique in that it was the first time a council had been called by the cardinals. Emperor Sigismund summoned another council to meet at Constance in 1414-1418. It dismissed the three existing popes and elected a new pope, Martin V. Early during the council the following decree was enacted:

> This holy Council of Constance...declares, first that
> it is lawfully assembled in the Holy Spirit, that it
> constitutes a General Council, representing the
> Catholic Church, and that therefore it has its author-
> ity immediately from Christ; and that all men, of ev-
> ery rank and condition, including the Pope himself,
> is bound to obey it in matters concerning the Faith,
> the abolition of the schism, and the reformation of
> the Church of God in its head and its members.
> Secondly it declares that anyone, of any rank and
> condition, who shall contumaciously refuse to obey
> the orders, decrees, statutes or instructions, made or
> to be made by this holy Council, or by any other
> lawfully assembled general council...shall, unless he
> comes to a right frame of mind, be subjected to fit-
> ting penance and punished appropriately: and if need
> be, recourse shall be had to the other sanctions of the
> law.2

This decree and its decision provide "evidence that it was the mind of the council that not only this particular Council of Constance but the General Council as such is the pope's superior."3

Accordingly, "The proceedings at Constance are a full and comprehensive rebuttal of the Vatican Decrees that the Pope is placed over the universal Church, that there is no superior authority to his, and that it is unlawful to appeal from his judgments to an Oecumenical Council as to a higher authority."[4]

The Council of Constance healed the schism. It was a victory for the conciliar movement, but the pope and the papalist party sought to undo the conciliar idea.

Pope Martin V (1415-1431) did not carry out the reforms he had promised. Under great pressure and very much against his will he was compelled to call a council to meet at Basel in 1431, but he died in that year and was succeeded by Eugene IV (1431-1447). His pontificate was chiefly devoted to an attempt to assert the supremacy of the papacy over the conciliar theory. The Council of Basel "was turned into a constitutional battle over papal absolutism and conciliar supremacy. This battle was fought with the pen as well as in debate."[5]

Pope Eugene issued three bulls against the council, but the emperor, Western Christendom, and most of the cardinals were against him and he was compelled to yield to their demands and revoke the bulls. Philip Schaff comments: "No revocation of a former decree could have been made more explicit. The Latin vocabulary was strained for words. Catholic historians refrain from making an argument against the plain meaning of the bull, which is fatal to the dogma of papal inerrancy and acknowledges the superiority of general councils."[6]

In spite of the pope's submission, the "civil war" continued inside the church. Its minority, together with the pope, transferred the Council to Florence in 1439. Here the prestige of the pope was increased by a temporary unification of the Eastern Church with the Western Church. The Eastern Church was pressed by the Turks and needed all the help it could muster, but in vain, for the Turks captured Constantinople in 1453. In the meantime, the majority in Basel deposed Pope Eugene and chose a new pope who declined to serve. Eugene won, and denounced the decrees of both Constance and Basel. Thus all hope was gone of "transforming the papacy into a constitutional monarchy or of effecting needed reform through conciliar action."[7]

But hope was to rise again in the person of Martin Luther and others who challenged the Roman church to restudy its catholicity and appealed for a general council to decide the future of the church.

THE COUNCIL OF TRENT

The Council of Trent was summoned in the mid-sixteenth century for the purpose of repudiating Protestantism, but it also became a platform for a fierce dispute between the papalist party and the conciliarists over the relationship of the bishops to the pope. As already noted, the conciliarists, with the early Church Fathers, held that the bishop of Rome is only the first among equals, while the papalists believed that the bishops received their authority from the pope who appoints them. The former likewise believed the council to be over the pope, but this the papalists denied. In the former group were the Spanish, French, and German bishops supported by their secular rulers. The emperor himself, although a Catholic and an opponent of Protestantism, believed in the principle affirmed by the Council of Constance, that a council is over the pope.

The "civil war" between papalists and conciliarists was characterized by disgraceful scenes during the council meetings as well as fighting in the streets with bloodshed and rival cries of "Hispania" and "Italia." Both groups were too strong to give in entirely. However, the pope's "tactics, which never varied during the whole period of the Council, and which were finally crowned with success were simple." T.M. Lindsay vividly describes the pope's diplomatic activities during the council:

> He maintained at all costs a numerical majority in the Synod ready to vote as he directed. This was done by systematic drafts of Italian Bishops to Trent. Many of the poorer ones were subsidized through Cardinal Sionetta, whose business it was to see that the mechanical majority was kept up, and to direct it how to vote. His Legates had the exclusive right of proposing resolutions; couriers took the proposals drafted by the various Congregations to Rome, and

the Pope revised them there before they were laid before the whole Council to be voted upon; spies informed him what were the objections of the French, Spanish, or German Bishops, and the Pope was diligent to bring all manner of influences to bear upon them to incline them to his mind; if he failed, he prevented the proposals being laid before the Council until he had counselled and bargained with the monarchs through special agents. The papal post-bags, containing proposed decrees or canons, went the round of the European Courts before they were presented to the Council, and the Bishops spoke and voted upon what had been already settled behind their backs and without their knowledge.[8]

At its last session the council "left entirely in the Pope's hands the confirmation of its decrees and the measures to be used for carrying them out."[9]

Less than a month after the close of the council (Dec. 4, 1563) Pope Pius IV issued a bull in which he claimed exclusive right to interpret its decrees, and within a year he made the Profession of the Tridentine Faith, or "Creed of Pius IV," binding on believers as a component part of the Catholic faith "without which no one can be saved" (Art. 12). Article 10 reads: "I acknowledge the holy Catholic Apostolic Roman Church for the mother and mistress of all churches; and I promise and swear true obedience to the Bishop of Rome, successor to St. Peter, Prince of the Apostles, and Vicar of Jesus Christ."[10]

GALLICANISM

A movement for an underground French church known as Gallicanism arose in France during the latter half of the seventeenth century. With roots in many similar attempts during previous centuries, its main purpose was to achieve freedom from papal authority. The Gallican Declaration, also known as the Five Gallican Articles, was formulated and approved by the Assembly of the French clergy on March 19, 1682.

The four main points of this Declaration have been outlined by Martin E. Marty: "1) pope and church have no power over temporal princes; 2) Constantinian decrees on the superiority of General Councils to popes remain; 3) local tradition demands care on the part of the papacy when it exercises authority; 4) the church must ratify papal decrees on matters of faith before these become permanent and absolute in their binding character."11

The Gallican Declaration was accepted by Louis XIV, but was condemned by Pope Alexander VIII (1690) and retracted by Louis XIV (1692) under Jesuit influence. It was, however, widely propagated during the eighteenth century and at the time of Napoleon again officially adopted. The Syllabus of Errors issued by Pius IX (1864) included a condemnation of Gallican principles when it states that it is an error that "national churches can be established, after being withdrawn and plainly separated from the authority of the Roman Pontiff."12 After Vatican I Gallicanism was further separated from Roman Catholicism but historically lived on in the Old Catholic movement that arose in Germany after Vatican I and will be noticed in that connection.

THE VATICAN I REVOLUTION

We have already seen how, century after century, a conflict raged within the Roman Catholic Church regarding papal supremacy. The climax came on July 18, 1870. Vatican Council I was in no sense universal. It was a council of the Roman Catholic Church alone, and not even truly representative of that part of Christendom. The numerical composition of the council and the constituencies they represented is a clear indication of that internal conflict.

Vatican I was the largest church council ever. During its first two sessions attendance at the Council of Trent never exceeded sixty-two and at the final session two hundred and fifty-five members signed the decrees. One thousand and thirty-seven prelates were entitled to attend Vatican Council I. Of these more than seven hundred were present at the opening meeting and within a short time their number increased to seven hundred and sixty-six. Of the total members five hundred and forty-one came from Europe, but a little more than half of these were from Italy. George Salmon illustrates the disproportion between the representatives of the various constituencies, which in turn influenced the final vote:

> There was no fair representation of bishops. In the first place, the assembly included some three hundred titular bishops—bishops not presiding over any real sees, but holding mere titles of honour given them by the Pope, or else missionary bishops deriving their titles from places where there were few or no Christian congregations....The twelve millions of Roman Catholics in Germany proper were represented at the Council by fourteen bishops; the seven hundred thousand inhabitants of the Papal States by sixty-two; three bishops of the minority—Cologne, Paris, and Cambray—represented five million; and these might be outvoted by any four of the seventy Neapolitan and Sicilian bishops.[13]

A.B. Hasler has brought to our attention that prior to Vatican I there was a "wait-and-see" attitude on the part of the curia and a majority of the bishops. Six years before Vatican I Pope Pius IX had polled and consulted some cardinals and bishops but found that within the Curia, as in general, there were reservations and resistance. But no matter what, the pope himself was determined to press for the dogma of infallibility. To support him "stood a small but unshakably resolute band of some fifty episcopal companions-in-arms." Their strength lay in the fact that they had the backing of the pope. But they could also count on the energetic support of a great number of Jesuits. "On the other side were about one hundred and thirty opponents of the definition and five hundred bishops who were at first undecided and indifferent."[14]

We are told that during the council there was no freedom of the press, for only material favoring the dogma was permitted to be published. "Such prominence of the Pope is characteristic of a Council convoked for the very purpose of proclaiming his personal infallibility, but is without precedent in history (except in some mediaeval Councils)."[15]

The introduction to the Canons and Dogmatic Decrees of the Council of Trent reads: "In the name of the Holy and Undivided Trinity, Father, and Son, and Holy Ghost. This sacred and holy, oecumenical, and general Synod of Trent,—[is] lawfully assembled."[16]   On the other hand the Dogmatic Decrees of the Vatican Council of 1870 begin with the name of the Pope: "Pius, Bishop, Servant of Servants of God."[17] The implication of the change in the introduction of the two documents is significant.

A large group of the members of the council protested the lack of freedom in the council sessions. "More than one hundred Prelates of all nations signed a strong protest (dated Rome, March 1, 1870) against the order of business, especially against the mere majority vote, and expressed the fear that in the end the authority of this Council might be impaired as wanting in truth and liberty—a calamity so direful in these uneasy times, that a greater could not be imagined. But this protest, like all the acts of the minority, was ignored."[18]

A verbal vote was taken on July 13, 1870. Four hundred fifty-one voted in the affirmative, sixty-two accepted the principle but did not agree to details, eighty-eight voted against, and eighty to ninety abstained from voting. There was no unanimous agreement on the vital dogma of infallibility.[19]

The day before the final vote fifty-six bishops wrote to the pope confirming their opposition, stating that they would stay away at the final session, and "sixty additional members of the opposition departed from Rome."[20]

The fateful moment arrived on July 18, 1870. In spite of all opposition the dogma of infallibility was passed with only two dissenting votes. With respect to those who later submitted to the papal autocracy, thus sacrificing their intellectual honesty, Philip Schaff wrote:

Johann Ignaz von Döllinger, one of if not the most learned German Roman Catholic of his day, predicted that if the doctrine of infallibility was decreed "it would present an incalculably weak point to the separated Churches—the Graeco-Russian and the Protestant. So far as can be foreseen, the whole controversy, as it has hitherto been carried on against the Catholic doctrine and Church, would concentrate itself more and more on this one doctrine."[21] Prior to the council Döllinger had written several articles on the history of the papacy. In one of these he wrote: "For us, the Catholic Church is in no way identical with papalism. Thus, notwithstanding outward Church communion, internally we are profoundly divided from those whose churchly ideal is a universal kingdom ruled spiritually and, where possible, even politically by a single monarch. This is a kingdom of compulsion and oppression."22

Many outstanding Roman Catholics had opposed the dogma, but Ignaz von Döllinger did not submit and did not sacrifice his intellectual honesty to papal autocracy. Returning from the council he wrote to Archbishop von Scherr:

> I cannot do so as a theologian, because the whole genuine tradition of the Church stands irreconcilably opposed to it. I cannot do so as an historian, because, as such, I know that the persistent endeavours to realise this theory of a universal sovereignty has cost Europe streams of blood, distracted and ruined whole countries, shaken to its foundations the beautiful organic edifice of the constitution of the older Church, and begotten, nursed, and maintained the worst abuses in the Church. Finally, I must reject it as a citizen, because, with its claims on the submission of States and monarchs and the whole political order of things to the papal power, and by the exceptional position claimed by it for the clergy, it lays the foundation for an endless and fatal discord between the State and the Church, between the clergy and the laity.23

After the council, Ignaz von Döllinger lent his influence to activities that led to the formation of Old Catholic churches in Germany, Switzerland, and Austria. Here, those who rejected the new dogma of papal infallibility were excommunicated and as a result founded their own bishoprics. The Old Catholic movement led to the organization of national churches, which united in the Union of Utrecht in 1889. An Old Catholic Church had been founded in the Netherlands back in the seventeenth century as a result of a dispute between the archbishop and the chapter of Utrecht. They fought for the preservation of their own ancient privileges and opposed Jesuit influence for complete control by Rome.

Bishoprics of the Old Catholic Church were also organized in Poland, Croatia, and Italy during the nineteenth century. While only a small part of Christendom, today, the Old Catholic Church reminds us of the inner conflict that has always been present within Roman Catholicism regarding papal supremacy and universal jurisdiction. The position of the Old Catholics remains the unofficial point of view in a large section of Roman Catholicism. Prior to Vatican II many clergy and theologians had hoped that the forthcoming council would, in some way or another, dilute the one-sided authority of the pope, especially in relation to the bishops. To Vatican II and this issue we will return later.

3

A CHURCH WITH A SOVEREIGN STATE AND SECULAR POWER

Roman Catholicism has as its head a person in whom religious and secular sovereignty are combined. How did this dual rulership develop? Why would a church insist on being a sovereign state as well?

The status of the papacy as a secular state and the Roman pontiff's claim to influence in secular and national affairs were both highlighted—by proponents and opponents alike—when the Vatican and President Reagan announced that official diplomatic relations were to be established between the United States and the Vatican. This new relationship was confirmed on January 10, 1984 by the appointment of William A. Wilson as the first American Ambassador to the Holy See.

Affirming its role as the only "true Catholic" church, the papacy is not only a church but also a state, and in performing its duties as a state, both internal and external, it is also a universal church. It is this two fold aspect of Roman Catholicism that, in a special way, makes it a riddle and causes what seems to be theological, ecclesiological, and political contradictions.

The ethos of the papacy, which led to official diplomatic relations with the United States, is the result of centuries of history and can only be understood in the light of that history. To the history of the origins, growth and vicissitudes of the Papal States, also called the States of the Church and the Patrimony of St. Peter, we will now turn.

EMPEROR CONSTANTINE:
Church Property and Organization

As Christianity grew and during the fourth century became the official religion in the form of an imperial state church, it acquired wealth and power and built up its own semi-political organization. As a result a new set of beliefs and attitudes in relation to political power began to grow. The church became more self-conscious, and a tendency developed to depreciate the importance of secular political authority and to exalt, by comparison, the spiritual authority of the church; this finally led to the concept that the church was not only the source of theology but also of law and secular power. The beginning of this development we find during the time of Emperor Constantine.

Having declared himself a Christian, Constantine's aim was to unite the secular state with the Christian church by the closest ties possible. By an edict, A.D. 321, he gave the church legal right to hold property, and enjoined observance of Sunday as the civil day of worship. He himself generously supported the church and its clergy, with money, buildings, and property. Following his example, wealthy families donated large estates outside of Rome and throughout Italy, by the fifth century making the church the largest landowner. Estates were also obtained outside Italy.

Another factor should be noticed. Emperor Constantine's recognition of the church and its subsequent association with the Roman state strongly influenced the practical organization of the church, which was made to conform to the civil organization of the empire. As Christianity spread there had come to be, generally, a bishop for each city, together with the territory attached to it. "The power and prestige of the clergy—the Christian *ordo*—increased as...the bishop became the most important figure in the life of the city and the representative of the whole community."1 Bishoprics were grouped into provinces, as the districts already were for civil purposes, and the bishop of the capital city of a province became the metropolitan, or archbishop of a diocese. "The logical culmination of this development was to make the capital of the Empire also the centre of the Church."2 In A.D. 326 Constantine moved to his new capital, Constantinople, and for some time the authority of the bishop of Rome was threatened not only by Antioch and Alexandria but also by the See of Constantinople. Eventually this move of the capital became an advantage to the bishop of Rome. He was no longer overshadowed by the emperor or even the imperial representatives, and as a result gained prestige. He became increasingly a person to be reckoned with in the affairs of the city. The bishop of Rome took over "vacated imperial prerogatives; it left him, for long periods, without a political rival in the West; as the imperial power in the West broke down, he emerged as the sole remaining symbol and source of authority."3 The absence of the emperor left Rome in the hands of the popes who gradually developed the temporal power and the States of the Church.

THE BARBARIAN INVASIONS:
The Bishop of Rome Gains Prestige

The origin of the temporal power of the pope and the estates of the church is closely related to the barbarian invasions in Italy and Western Europe. Thus the papal state made its beginning on the ruins of Western Europe. In the dark hour when Rome was sacked by Alaric in A.D. 410, we find Pope Innocent virtually "governor" of the city.

As the empire declined during the fifth century, the bishop of Rome became the representative of the Roman tradition and carried it over into the sphere of the Christian religion, which thus became Romanized. This is illustrated in the work of Pope Leo the Great, A.D. 440-461. Addressing the Romans on the Feast of Sts. Peter and Paul, he could say: "These [Peter and Paul] are they, who have brought thee to such glory as a holy nation, a chosen people, a royal and priestly city that thou mightest be made the head of the world by the Holy See of St. Peter."4

Pope Gregory the Great, A.D. 590-604, was not only the spiritual head of Western Europe but also virtually king of Italy. "In the person of Gregory the Bishop of Rome first became, in act and in influence, if not in avowed authority, a temporal sovereign."5

The further development of papal supremacy is closely related to the Islamic conquest. The progress of Islam was extraordinary. Within a decade after Mohammed's death in A.D. 632, the Moslems conquered Syria, Palestine, Persia, and Egypt. Carthage was captured in A.D. 698 and the invasion of Spain began in A.D. 711. Constantinople was besieged in A.D. 668 but as yet in vain. The Islamic conquest reduced to insignificance three of the four eastern apostolic Sees: Antioch, Jerusalem, and Alexandria. The See of Constantinople was weakened and the African church, long crippled, came utterly to an end. As the Eastern Empire and the Eastern Church were thus diminished, the See of Rome became the main representative of Christendom, and this position was further strengthened as the church gained new territory in the West.

In England the old Celtic Christianity was suppressed, its adherents persecuted and to a large degree exterminated by the invading barbarians from Northern Europe who settled in the occupied territory. The work of Christianizing these barbarians and winning over the remaining Celtic Christians to Rome was begun by Augustine, a monk whom Pope Gregory the Great sent to England. Gradually the Roman form of Christianity won its way over most of the British Isles. In Germany, Boniface (A.D. 680-755), a native of England, brought Christianity into subjection to Rome. Boniface was in constant correspondence with the popes, whose decisions he sought and followed in all difficulties. Of him it is said, "He hated every feature of individuality and national independence in matters of the church. To him true Christianity was identical with Romanism, and he made Germany as loyal to the Pope as was his native England....Those who labored without papal authority were to him dangerous hirelings, thieves and robbers who climbed up some other way."6

THE DOGMA OF THE TWO POWERS

The starting point for an understanding of medieval church-and-state relations is the dogma of the two powers, the spiritual and the temporal. The medieval popes sought reconciliation between the two powers and their objective appealed, philosophically, to the medieval mind, which looked upon the universe as a unity. Otto Gierke points out that "Political Thought when it is genuinely medieval starts from the Whole, but ascribes an intrinsic value to every

Partial Whole down to and including the Individual." But since the individual is part of the whole, "the Constitutive Principle of the Universe is in the first place Unity. God, the absolute One, is before and above all the World's Plurality, and is the one source and one goal of every Being."7 When "an External, Visible Community comprehending All Mankind" was postulated it followed that

> in all centuries of the Middle Age Christendom, which in destiny is identical with Mankind, is set before us as a single, universal Community, founded and governed by God Himself. Mankind is one 'mystical body'; it is one single and internally connected 'people' or 'folk'; it is an all embracing corporation (*universitas*), which constitutes that Universal Realm, spiritual and temporal, which may be called the Universal Church (*ecclesia universalis*), or, with equal propriety, the Commonwealth of the Human Race (*respublica generis humani*). Therefore that it may attain its one purpose, it needs One Law (*lex*) and One Government (*unicus principatus*).8

The papal party sought to solve the problem of the two powers by asserting the sovereignty of the spiritual power. One argument for sacerdotal pre-eminence was the theocratic Jewish state of antiquity; another, that the saving of the soul was more important than the regulation of man's earthly life. A third argument arose out of the fact that the king is only a layman. Therefore it was claimed that the church had the right to condemn and punish any evildoing on his part and to decide what acts of his were evil. Furthermore, the state is of earthly and not, as is the church, of heavenly origin.

Prior to the pontificate of Gregory VII the relationship between the *sacerdotium* (priesthood) and the *regnum* (civil authority) had been formulated by St. Peter Damian (1007-1072) and Cardinal Humbert (d. 1061). Damian expressed a close union between the two:

> "The King shall be found in the Roman Pontiff, the Roman Pontiff in the King", for, as he said, "in one Mediator of God and man, these two, the *regnum*

and the *sacerdotium*, are bound together by a divine mystery."…Yet even Damian had believed the Roman Church to be superior, not only to every other ecclesiastical authority, but to every lay power also.9

Cardinal Humbert used the analogy of soul and body as expressing the relationship between the religious and the secular powers. "It was for the spiritual power, as the directing force of the body of Christendom, to decide what should be done, for the temporal to put the decisions into effect."10 Another medieval comparison was that of the sun and the moon. As the sun excelled the moon so the *sacerdotium* excelled the *regnum*. Having pointed out that from the time of Gregory VII it was demonstrated "that all policial arrangements should be regarded as part and parcel of the ecclesiastical organization" Otto Gierke writes:

> If Mankind be only one, and if there can be but one State that comprises all Mankind, that State can be no other than the Church that God Himself has founded, and all temporal lordship can be valid only in so far as it is part and parcel of the Church. Therefore the Church, being the one true State, has received by a mandate from God the plenitude of all spiritual and temporal powers, they being integral parts of One Might. The Head of this all-embracing State is Christ. But, as the Unity of Mankind is to be realized already in this world, His celestial kingship must have a terrestrial presentment. As Christ's Vice-Regent, the earthly Head of the Church is the one and only Head of all Mankind. The Pope is the wielder of what is in principle an Empire (*principatus*) over the Community of Mortals. He is their Priest and their King; their spiritual and temporal Monarch; their Lawgiver and Judge in all causes supreme.11

The medieval solution to the unity of mankind thus expressed has much in common with Catholic ecumenism. (The latter will be dealt with in another connection.) Then and now the theological framework is the same.

The breakdown of the Roman Empire and the rapid spread of Christianity finally led to a situation in which the bishop of Rome, now head of the Western Church, had at times more prestige and power than the kings of the Christian nations. Thus it was that in "the Middle Ages the Church was not a State, it was the State; the State, or rather the civil authority (for a separate society was not recognized), was merely the police department of the Church." Historian John N. Figgis continues by saying that the church "took over from the Roman Empire its theory of the absolute and universal jurisdiction of the supreme authority, and developed it into the doctrine of the *plenitudo potestatis* of the Pope."12

During the Middle Ages the church took over the vacated prerogatives of the Roman Empire. It became a political institution. The sword was used for the church and by its direction. This is illustrated by the Crusades, which transferred the leadership of Europe from the emperor to the pope, and directly influenced the development of papal supremacy. The importance of the Crusades as a means to further the cause of the papacy is well expressed by George A. Campbell: "The first Crusade was a desperate expedient to restore the lost authority of the Church. Its success was beyond [Pope] Urban's wildest imaginings."13

The immediate effect of the Crusades was to open up "new fields of ambition to the hierarchy, to stimulate wonderfully their power for political organization. It was this impulse that gave birth to the Crusades, and that enabled the Popes, stepping forth as the rightful leaders of a religious war, to bend it to serve their own ends."14

The image of the pope was further enhanced by the coronation of the emperors by the pope. It gave the appearance that the pope bestowed the imperial power on the one of his choice. Thus the coronation of Charlemagne on Christmas Day of the year A.D. 800 is called "the central event of the Middle Ages," and "one of those very few events of which, taking them simply, it may be said that if they had not happened, the history of the world would have been different."15 While Charlemagne considered the pope his highest prelate, the general impression of the coronation that remained in the mind of the succeeding generation was the picture of the pope placing the crown on the head of a kneeling king. "Such a sight as that of an emperor being crowned by a Pope had never been seen before. The basilica of St. Peter was henceforth regarded as the cradle of the empire, which owed its rebirth to the Apostolic Vicar, the Pope."[16] For the pope the act of coronation became a final declaration of independence from the Eastern emperor as the legal ruler of Rome. In the view of Alcuin (an adviser to Charlemagne), who seemed to have had a part in the scheme of the coronation, "the pope occupied the first, the emperor the second, the king the third degree in the scale of earthly dignities."[17]

THE BIRTH OF THE STATES OF THE CHURCH

The actual beginning of the papal state can be told briefly. A new controversy between Rome and the Eastern Empire opened in A.D. 726. Emperor Leo III (A.D. 717-741), also called the Isaurian, issued in that year a decree against the reverence paid to icons, that is, religious images and pictures. Germanus, the patriarch of Constantinople, opposed the emperor and laid down his episcopal dignity, and Anastasius, one of the emperor's followers, was consecrated as patriarch. Pope Gregory II (A.D. 715-731), wrote a violent letter to the emperor opposing the decree.

His successor, Pope Gregory III (A.D. 731-741), continued to resist Leo III. On his part, the emperor sent out a fleet to punish the pope, Rome, and Italy, but the fleet suffered shipwreck. In his anger Leo severed that part of the Eastern Empire which was under papal jurisdiction from the pope and subjected it to the patriarch of Constantinople. This loss for the papacy was amply compensated for by the fact that the papacy now found itself independent of the emperor. Now the Romans found the pope their only ruler. Isolated from all help from the emperor and threatened by the Lombards in northern Italy, the papacy turned to the Carolingians.

The further development of the papal power was closely associated with the growth of the Carolingian dynasty among the Franks. Charles Martel had defeated the Moslems in A.D. 732, but refused to help Pope Gregory III, in A.D. 739, against the Lombards. However, his son Pepin sought the advice of the pope in regard to the question whether he, rather than the Merovingians, was not the rightful ruler of France. The pope answered in the affirmative, and thus authorized the usurpation. In A.D. 751 Pepin was anointed like the kings of Israel. The pope had helped Pepin, and before long Pepin was asked to help the pope.

In A.D. 751 the Lombard king, Aistulf, captured Ravenna, which was the seat of the exarchate, the representative of the emperor, whose court was in Constantinople. Pope Stephen II (A.D. 752-757), isolated from the emperor on account of the iconoclastic controversy and failing to win from Aistulf any concession, crossed the Alps that he might ask for Pepin's support. Pepin and his lords promised to help the pope. Stephen anointed Pepin together with his two sons.

Pepin took an army to Italy and defeated the pope's enemies in A.D. 754. On account of a new rising of the Lombards, Pepin once more appeared, invoked by a letter written in the name of Peter. The letter reads:

> I, Peter the Apostle, have been set by the power of Christ, the son of the living God, to be a light to the whole world....To this apostolic Roman Church of God, entrusted to me, your hope of future reward is attached. And so, I who have adopted you as sons, call on you, to defend this Roman state from the hands of its enemies....Give help to my people of Rome now, that I may be able to help you hereafter at the day of judgment....by the hands of my vicar, I have entrusted to you, to be delivered, from its enemies, the Church, which the Lord has given into my keeping....If you come quickly to my aid, then, helped by my prayers, you will, after overcoming your enemies in this life, and being happy here, enjoying the gifts of eternal life, but if, as I trust you will not, you delay your assistance, know that you are cut off from eternal life.[18]

The letter had its desired effect. Pepin came back with his army, and the Lombard power was effectively broken in A.D. 755.

What now followed is of the highest importance in connection with the temporal power of the pope. Pepin "declared to the ambassadors of the East who demanded the restitution of Ravenna and its territory to the Byzantine empire, that his sole object in the war was to show his veneration for St. Peter." All the cities and land which Aistulf surrendered were given to the Apostolic See. This meant that the pope became the undisputed sovereign not only of Rome but also of the exarchate of Ravenna, and thus actual ruler over a large part of Italy. "This donation of Pepin is the foundation of 'the Patrimony of St. Peter.'"19 While the pope had previously exercised temporal rulership, he had been responsible in theory to the emperor through the imperial representative, who had his court in Ravenna. But now the pope himself was the actual ruler. Therefore, rulership of the pope in and through his own state dates from A.D. 756 and continued until 1870, and then again since 1929.

During the reign of the Carolingians the Roman faith was the cementing bond of the empire. When the Carolingian empire was divided into three parts in A.D. 843, the division weakened the power of the secular rulers as compared with that of the papacy. Modern France and Germany owe their origin to the division of A.D. 843.

FORGERY AND THE STATES OF THE CHURCH

The beginning of the territorial sovereignty of the pope is related to some famous forgeries. One of the most important of these is the "Donation of Constantine," which has been called the "cornerstone of papal power."20 This document dates back to the beginning of the year A.D. 744; it was manufactured at Rome, probably at the Lateran.21 Basic to the Donation of Constantine was "the *Legenda sancti Silvestrei*, a somewhat romantic version of Constantine's conversion made towards the end of the fifth century."22 The Sylvester-Constantine legend narrates how Pope Sylvester healed Constantine from leprosy and Constantine in return "conferred on the Roman Church the privilege whereby it was the head of all the priests within the Roman world, just as the judges had their head in the person of the king."23

What the *Legenda* hinted at was fully expressed by the Donation of Constantine, as illustrated by the following passages from the Donation:

> To the most holy and blessed father of fathers Sylvester, bishop of the city of Rome and pope, and to all his successors the pontiffs who are about to sit upon the chair of St. Peter until the end of time...(Peter) is seen to have been constituted vicar of the Son of God, so the pontiffs, who are the representatives of that same chief of the apostles, should obtain from us and our empire the power of a supremacy greater than the earthly clemency of our imperial serenity is seen to have had conceded to it,...we decree that his holy Roman church shall be honoured with veneration; and that, more than our empire and earthly throne, the most sacred seat of St. Peter shall be gloriously exalted; we giving to it the imperial power, and dignity of glory, and vigour and honour....he shall have the supremacy as well over the four chief seats...as also over all the churches of God in the whole world....behold we—giving over to the oft-mentioned most blessed pontiff, our father Sylvester the universal pope, as well our palace, as has been said, as also the city of Rome and all the provinces, districts and cities of Italy or of the western regions; and relinquishing them, by our inviolable gift, to the power and sway of himself or the pontiffs his successors.24

For seven centuries this "most stupendous of all mediaeval forgeries" commanded "the unquestioning belief of mankind."25 It gave an effective antiquity to the high concepts of papal supremacy. It made Justinian's decree of A. D. 533 appear as only a renewal of a decree already given by the first Christian emperor, Constantine. It also made null the decisions of the first four general councils, which only granted the bishop of Rome power in his own province and denied the right of the clergy in other provinces to appeal to Rome. Rome, as capital of the empire, automatically bestowed importance on its bishop, to whom the provinces appealed as naturally as they did to the emperor.

Sometime before the middle of the ninth century other forgeries, the Pseudo-Isidorian Decretals, were composed. The decretals went under the false name of Bishop Isidor of Seville, who died in A.D. 636. There is no agreement as to who the author of the decretals was, but scholars agree that the work was done by some ecclesiastic in the church of France and constitutes "to a large extent a conscious high church fraud."26

The Pseudo-Isidorian Decretals consist of a collection of church laws, in the main genuine, and a great number of letters by the popes, most of them forgeries. Bringing the latter together with genuine material, made the former look authentic. The collection also includes the Donation of Constantine. During the Renaissance this work was demonstrated to be false. While Catholic scholars recognize its spuriousness, they maintain that the principles expressed are valid.

POPE NICHOLAS THE GREAT
AND SECULAR POWER

The immediate result of the Pseudo-Isidorian Decretals is seen in the pontificate of Nicholas I (A.D. 858-867), also styled the Great. He made full use of the political situation and claimed the papal supremacy as it was advocated in the Pseudo-Isidorian Decretals. This is illustrated in three events which mark his pontificate. The first event has to do with the patriarch of Constantinople. Ignatius was deposed by the emperor, and Photius elected in his place. Both Ignatius and Photius appealed to Rome. Nicholas decided in favor of Ignatius, but failed in his attempt to reinstate Ignatius. In the controversy which followed, the Greek and Latin churches were further alienated before the complete separation in 1054. Nicholas, in his letters to Photius and Emperor Michael III, expressed the idea of papal supremacy in unsurpassed words, but in full accord with the Pseudo-Isidorian Decretals. A few statements from his letters give a vivid description of the papal claim: "No decision must be given on any new matter that arises without the consent of the Roman See and the Roman Pontiff." Having confessed to Peter, he continues: "After him, his vicars, sincere servers of God, free from the mists which are wont to cause men to wander from the right path, have received the same privilege, and have steadily persevered in the government of the Lord's sheep which has been entrusted to them."27 He says further:

> These privileges, by the words of Christ, founded on Blessed Peter, ever reverenced in the Church, cannot be lessened or changed; for human efforts cannot move the foundation which God has laid....The privileges of this See existed before your empire, they will remain after you, and they will remain inviolate as long as Christianity shall be preached.28

As previously noted, the supremacy thus expressed by Nicholas failed in this case but it later achieved its desired result. We recall that Lothaire II, king of Lorraine, had divorced his wife and married his mistress.29 Lothaire's wife appealed to the pope, who declared void the sanction to the divorce issued by the archbishops of Trier and Cologne; he excommunicated them and compelled the king to take back his wife. Hincmar, the archbishop of Rheims, complained that the pope, "makes himself the emperor of the whole world."30

Hincmar himself was soon to feel the power of Nicholas. He had deposed Rothad, bishop of Soissons, and with the help of Charles the Bald, grandson of Charlemagne, put Rothad in prison. Thereupon Rothad appealed to the pope, who called him to Rome and reinstated him. In order to prove his authority over a king and a bishop who would not reinstate Rothad, the Pope quotes the Pseudo-Isidorian Decretals. We are told that "Hincmar protested against the validity of the new decretals and their application to France, and the protest lingered for centuries in the Gallican liberties till they were finally buried in the papal absolutism of the Vatican Council of 1870."31

The pontificate of Pope Nicholas I marks the climax of papal power for the next two centuries.

THE PAPACY OFF THE PRECIPICE

Causes of the sudden and long continued downfall of papal power, after the height to which Nicholas brought it, can "be found in weak, wicked, worldly Popes, in anarchy and political confusion in Italy, and in feudalism." As a result "the Church was reaping the reward of a close alliance with the state. All the gains made by the Church during this epoch were of a secular character. The moral and spiritual powers of Latin Christianity lay dormant beneath a mass of corruption, self-seeking and worldly passions which covered them and nearly extinguished them."[32]

Degeneration overtook the church in all its functions. The bishoprics were mainly hereditary, and offices, ordination, and the usual rites of religion could only be obtained through payment. In other words, the Roman Church had become a political institution. The mingling of temporal supremacy with spiritual supremacy inevitably compromised the spiritual authority. This so much more since the popes' temporal rulership, generally speaking, was not superior to that of the secular rulers.

The degradation into which the papacy plunged shortly after Nicholas I can hardly be described. For some years one pope followed another as the creation of rival mobs of the city of Rome. For example, in eight years nine popes succeeded one another and in several cases suffered violent death at the hands of their opponents. Then for some years the papacy was "the Reign of Harlots." The Roman noble Theophylact and his two daughters, Theodora and Marozia, gave this name to the papacy. Pope John XI (A.D. 931-936), was a son of Marozia. Alberio, her other son, ruled Rome and controlled papal elections. Pope John XII (A.D. 955-963), Alberic's son, was made pope at the age of seventeen or eighteen.

Duchesne describes the vice and wickedness of John XII: "His illicit amours were a matter of public knowledge, for they were restrained neither by ties of blood nor by respect of persons."[33] When John XII felt his power threatened by Berenger II, the new Italian monarch, he asked Otto of Germany for help. Otto saw an opportunity to extend his power and with an overpowering force he conquered Italy and was acclaimed its king. After taking an oath to acknowledge and protect the Holy See and the freedom of

Rome, he was crowned emperor by Pope John II in A.D. 962. Thus began the so-called Holy Roman Empire, which lasted until 1806. From now on the history of the papacy is interlocked with that of the empire. The popes were nominated by the emperors with little or no regard to their personal fitness.

Before the middle of the eleventh century three popes were contesting with one another for the papal chair. The German emperor, Henry II (1039-1056), now interfered and banished all three. A synod in Rome granted Henry "the right of nominating the supreme pontiff," the reason being that "the Roman priesthood, who had forfeited the respect of the world even more by habitual simony than by the flagrant corruption of their manners, were forced to receive German after German as their bishop, at the bidding of a ruler so powerful, so severe, and so pious."34 Emperor Henry III rescued the papacy, but he and his successors found the papacy, in its quest for temporal power, to be their worst enemy.

POPE GREGORY VII:
The Papacy Up Again from the Precipice

In the moral rebuilding of the papacy the monastic order of Cluny was prominent. This monastic order was not under episcopal or secular jurisdiction but directly under the protection of the pope.

In their form of organization "the Cluniacs became the nearest approach then conceivable to what the Jesuits were to become several centuries later—an autocratically ruled society of men within the Church."35 It is therefore natural that at the height of its temporal power the papacy was ruled by men who came from this "autocratically ruled society of men." Pope Gregory VII (1073-1085) was guided by the ideals of the monastic order of Cluny where he had served. To a large degree Gregory VII succeeded in realizing the lofty ideals of *Dictatus Papae*, which granted absolute power to the pope.

Gregory sent Cardinal Hugo Candidus to Spain, reminding the rulers that "the whole kingdom of Spain was, and had been from the olden time, part and parcel of the patrimony of St. Peter." It was added, that "*no territories once annexed to the church could be withdrawn from her* by any act of human authority, or any pressure of external circumstances."[36] Normans who invaded Italy bound themselves to the pope "by an oath of civil allegiance, *irrespective of the supremacy of the empire*, over the territories he occupied." In central Italy the pope had control "through the devoted attachment of the countesses Beatrix and Mathilda of Tuscany."[37] In short, it may be said of Gregory: "No region was too remote or too barbarous not to come within his idea of ecclesiastical unity and of papal suzerainty."[38] No wonder that Gregory VII has been styled a world ruler.

THE PAPACY AT ITS HEIGHT AND THE SEQUEL

Pope Innocent III (1198-1216), brought the papacy to its actual height. Dealing with the relationship between the papacy and the empire he wrote:

> The Creator of the universe set up two great luminaries in the firmament of heaven; the greater light to rule the day, the lesser light to rule the night. In the same way for the firmament of the universal Church, which is spoken of as heaven, he appointed two great dignities; the greater to bear rule over souls,...the lesser to bear rule over bodies....These dignities are the pontifical authority and the royal power. Furthermore, the moon derives her light from the sun, and is in truth inferior to the sun in both size and quality, in position as well as effect. In the same way the royal power derives its dignity from the pontifical authority.[39]

When it comes to imperial elections Innocent III acknowledges that the right belongs to the princes. "But the princes should recognize, and assuredly do recognize, that the right and authority to examine the person so elected king (to be elevated to the Empire) belongs to us who anoint, consecrate and crown him."[40]

As expressed by Innocent III, the temporal power of the pope had its source in the pope's spiritual supremacy as the Vicar of Jesus Christ. The monarchs of Europe experienced this autocracy in a literal sense. At the death of Emperor Henry VI in 1197, Germany was divided between Philip of Swabia and Otto of Brunswick. Innocent played the one against the other and received concessions from both. Finally, the young son of Henry VI was put forward by the pope and chosen as Frederick II. Innocent thus dictated the imperial succession. In turn Frederick II confirmed the papal sovereignty of the territory from coast to coast in central Italy.

In his dealings with France, Innocent upheld the cause of morality and justice even in the case of the king. Philip had unjustly divorced his wife, and for this sin the country was placed under interdict and Philip was compelled to take back his queen.

> The third great power in Europe was England. Here, the pope set aside King John's candidate as archbishop. When John resisted, he laid England under an interdict, excommunicated the king and declared his throne forfeited. John submitted to the pope and acknowledged the pope as the temporal overlord of England. During the twelfth and thirteenth centuries the popes competed with the Hohenstaufen emperors over the temporal supremacy of Europe. The papacy sought to destroy the Hohenstaufens and thus gain full temporal supremacy. The misfortune of Emperor Frederick II (1215-1250), was that he gave "the Popes a hold over him which they well knew how to use....With Frederick fell the Empire."41 One historian writes: With the overthrow of the Hohenstaufen emperors, the Pope stood forth in strong relief as the sole heir and representative of the claim of ancient Rome to universal rule. This universality of papal supremacy was not only ably defended by keen ecclesiastical jurists, by the canon law, by the legislation of numerous councils, and by many historical precedents; but also by the brainiest theologians of the thirteenth century, such as Albertus Magnus, Duns Scotus, and Thomas Aquinas, who sought to prove that submis-

sion to the Roman Pontiff was required of every human being.42

Before the end of the thirteenth century the papal states were divided into five regions for administrative purposes, and at the same time great noble families began to exercise influence and control over the cities and provinces. In his broader plans for unifying Italy under his leadership Boniface VIII (1294-1303) sought to exercise authority in all the provinces.

It looked as if the papacy was triumphing, but under the surface forces developed as a reaction against the temporal supremacy of the pope. Even the pontificates of the great popes were full of defeats. Gregory VII, who humiliated Henry IV at Canossa, died in exile. The pontificate of Innocent III is said to have been "in one sense the greatest of medieval achievements," in another, "the greatest of medieval failures."43 Boniface VIII, who expressed the highest claim of papal supremacy, died as a captive in the Vatican. Then followed the Babylonian Captivity of the popes (1309-1377), when the popes resided in Avignon in France, as absentee landlords of the papal states. Accordingly, the secular authority rested in the hands of the local nobility. The same was the case during the period of the Papal Schism (1378-1417) where we find two lines of popes, one residing in Rome and the other in Avignon, each competing for the loyalty of Europe.

The creation of the new national states in the fourteenth and fifteenth centuries curtailed exercise of the temporal powers of the papacy. However, popes such as Julius II (1503-1513) and Leo X (1513-1521) re-established a centralized monarchy of the States of the Church, but the papacy was controlled by a number of families out of which the popes were elected. The States of the Church were an object of rivalry among these families, and at the same time there was outside control by either Austria or the Spanish Hapsburgs. Such was the historical situation until Napoleon conquered Italy in 1797. The following year his General Berthier took Pope Pius VI into exile, where he died. Napoleon declared the Papal States a part of the Roman Republic, but at the Congress of Vienna, in 1814, they were re-established and continued for half a century.

When all the historical facts are taken into consideration, the claim of temporal supremacy and the sovereignty of the States of the Church became the Achilles' heel of Roman Catholicism. Many Catholics, past and present, are embarrassed and concerned over the secular aspects of their church. The use and results of the temporal power of the papacy appear, generally speaking, not to be better than any of those of the secular kingdoms "of this world."

4

VATICAN DIPLOMACY

When one attempts to penetrate the riddle of Roman Catholicism he is reminded about Winston Churchill's nine-word description of Russia: "A riddle wrapped in a mystery inside an enigma." The riddle is concealed in the pope, who unites in himself both spiritual and temporal powers. It is, therefore, impossible to draw a line between the boundaries of his spiritual and temporal aims and activities.

The States of the Vatican, over which the pope had sovereignty, existed from A.D. 756 to 1870, except for a brief interruption during the Napoleanic wars when the French tricolored flag was raised atop the castle of St. Angelo. The Italian struggle for national unity during the nineteenth century eventually led to the establishment of the kingdom of Italy under Victor Emmanuel, in 1861, and included the papal territories in Italy except for Rome and its vicinity. In 1870, however, the king captured Rome and the city voted for annexation to Italy. Pope Pius IX declared himself prisoner of the Vatican and excommunicated the king, asserting that he could not exercise his papal prerogatives without territorial independence. To the French ambassador he said, "All that I want is a small corner of earth where I am master. This is not to say that I would refuse my States if they were offered me. But so long as I do not have this little corner of earth I shall not be able to exercise in their fullness my spiritual functions."[1]

It is ironic that the loss of the Vatican State took place two months after Pope Pius IX had declared the dogma of papal infallibility during Vatican Council I. It has been suggested that one reason for proclaiming the dogma of infallibility was the anxiety to preserve the state of the church. It was hoped "that no one would

48

dare to take action against a pope whose infallibility had been solemnly proclaimed *urbi et orbi* in ecumenical council."2 But the pope lost his sovereign state and had none for nearly sixty years.

THE STATE OF VATICAN CITY

By the Treaty of the Lateran in 1929 Pope Pius XI entered into an agreement with the Fascist leader Mussolini that gave the pope sovereign jurisdiction over Vatican City, the Lateran, and the papal summer residence at Castle Gandolfo as well as certain office buildings in Rome classified as extra-territorial. In return the pope recognized the government of Mussolini. The pope was now again a temporal sovereign in an unchallenged and independent territory. Financial compensation was also made for the loss of the papal territories in 1870. Robert A. Graham, S.J., expresses the Roman Catholic view of the treaty when he writes:

> But the recovery and peaceful possession of this civil sovereignty was more than a simple paragraph in international chronology. It was a vindication of the papal claims that such sovereignty was due it in virtue of the special mission the Holy See must perform in the world. For, during the long years of conflict, the issue had become glaringly clear: the papacy wanted back the temporal power, not as any dethroned prince seeks the restoration of his crown unjustly taken from him, but in the name of the independence it needed as the organ of a universal Church. International law, by recognizing the statehood of the State of Vatican City, recognizes implicitly the legitimacy of this claim. At least it reconciles itself to acknowledge as inevitable a situation it does not fully understand and to which it is not fully sympathetic.3

The State of Vatican City (*Lo Stato della Citta del Vaticano*) occupies 108.7 acres and has a population of about one thousand, yet it has all the components of a sovereign state. It maintains ministries, has its own flag, currency, stamps, police, and official newspaper, *Osservatore Romano*, and a radio station with programs transmitted in many languages. The Vatican State is an absolute monarchy and theocracy with the pope, Vicar of Christ, as its absolute sovereign. Notice the following description of his sovereignty: "All laws are a sovereign emanation of the will of the pope, who is the ultimate source of all power, even though this is at times delegated to others for practical reasons. The pope alone has the fullness of legislative, executive, and judicial power and represents Vatican City in international relations."4 Roman Catholic scholars hold that the nearly sixty years' lack of papal territorial sovereignty (1870 to 1929) proved to be an advantage for the pope. Robert A. Graham explains:

> Without the dramatization of the Roman question over a sustained period of time the present tiny territorial sovereignty would lack much of the authenticity now conceded to it. It was necessary during those years not only to justify the claim in theory but also to impress its merits first upon Italy and secondly upon the other states. The Pope had to act as a king before the world community would recognize him as one. The ultimate triumph of the papacy is all the greater because it had to convince a modern world cool and even hostile to the sight of a prelate at the head of any temporal government, especially when that temporal government is entirely subordinated to the needs of a world religion.5

The uniqueness of the State of Vatican City lies in the fact that it has at its head one who is the spiritual leader of approximately 800 million Roman Catholic believers around the globe. We will now consider briefly the relation between the Vatican State and the Holy See, and their relation to Roman Catholics world-wide and diplomatic relations with the nations of the world.

MODERN PAPAL DIPLOMACY

The Vatican is a unique institution, being both a church and a state. The State of Vatican City and the Holy See, also referred to as the Apostolic See, are two distinct entities recognized as such by international law. The Holy See is the supreme spiritual organ and administrative organization of the Roman Catholic Church with the pope as the head, but he is also the temporal ruler of Vatican City; the two are therefore indissolubly united in him as a person. Actually, Vatican City exists for the purposes of the Holy See, that is, for the sake of the pope and the church. The New Catholic Encyclopedia expresses it in these words: "This state was created with temporal sovereignty primarily to assure independence of spiritual action to the Holy See. Vatican City is thus a means to a higher end, an instrument of another pre-existing juridical subject, from which it cannot be separated. The close union with the Holy See imports to this minuscule state its great importance; it also makes it juridically and politically unique in the world."[6]

In an address to diplomats accredited to the Holy See, Pope Pius XII spoke about the *raison d'etre* of Vatican City in these words: "It was created to ensure the absolute freedom and independence of the Holy See and to guarantee its indisputable sovereignty, even in the international field, in the spiritual government of the Catholic Church in the whole world, and to constitute a visible sign of such absolute freedom, independence and sovereignty." While the Vatican City state is merely a dot on the map of nations of the world, it is "nevertheless, in the spiritual order...a symbol of great value and of universal extension, for it is the guarantee of the absolute independence of the Holy See in the accomplishment of its world-wide mission."[7] The pope also pointed out that in spite of the smallness of the territory it is "singled out by Providence for its great moral value, and for the strength and significance of its influence, is one of the focal points around which the history of the world gravitates, a reality without which all the evolution of the past would be but an inexplicable riddle." On account of this the pope felt that it was "no vain boast to say that this tiny Vatican territory, with all it contains in the reality of today and in the memories of its past, is like a citadel of peace and reconciliation in the midst of the terrible happenings of our times, a great hope for the future and a solid support which many people look up to even those who live apart from the Church."8

A month before the second Vatican Council closed Pope Paul VI addressed the United Nations General Assembly, describing himself as "the 'least-invested'among the representatives of sovereign States with a minuscule, as it were symbolic, temporal sovereignty, only as much as is necessary to be free to exercise his spiritual mission, and to assure all those who deal with him that he is independent of every other sovereignty of this world."9

While Vatican City is subordinated to the Holy See and ambassadors are accredited not to the former but to the latter, it is acknowledged that the pope could not claim the prerogatives of a temporal ruler without the Vatican City State. Referring to the international juristic personality of the Catholic Church and the Lateran Treaty, Cardinal Hyginus Eugene, apostolic nuncio to Belgium and the European Economic Council, writes that the latter "merely once more provided the Pope, who is the spiritual sovereign of the Church, with another title to sovereignty, that of temporal sovereignty, which would immediately cease to exist if the Vatican State became extinct."10

Non-Roman Catholics consider this situation and church-state relationship as an anomaly and a riddle, but Roman Catholics see in it the unique position of their church. Catholic scholars admit this anomaly and uniqueness. At the same time they admit that recognition of the Vatican State implies recognition of the moral and spiritual realities of the Roman Catholic Church and its head, the pope. Dealing with the unique position of papal diplomacy in international law, one writes: "The states deal with the Holy See as they deal with one another and as they do not deal with any other non-state institution. They would continue to maintain this attitude even if the Pope were not the temporal ruler of the Vatican State. This was demonstrated from 1870 to 1929 when the Pope was not generally regarded as a temporal sovereign."11 Cardinal Eugene expresses the same concept but with different emphasis: "Although international juridical regulation holds fast to the fundamental principle of the absolute equality before the law of all members of the international community, the Catholic Church and the Holy See are by courtesy generally accorded a special consideration because of their spiritual mission and of the moral values which they proclaim, promote and defend."12

It is suggested that the countries which have accredited a papal nuncio (ambassador) from the Holy See recognize the juxtaposition of the Vatican City and the Holy See by the fact that the papal nuncio is always the dean (head) of all the accredited ambassadors. He has the first rank and presides when the ambassadors are together for official functions, and he is their spokesman if they, as a body, have taken an action. On this point Robert A. Graham makes an interesting comparison: "The sovereignty of the Pope also, in its turn, is a product of the ceremonial hierarchy developed during the Middle Ages. The precedence of the Pope over the emperor and all crowned heads implied at the same time the precedence of papal nuncios over representatives of all other princes."13

History indicates that, during certain periods and in different circumstances, nations perceive their diplomatic relation with the pope as a temporal sovereign, and at other times as a spiritual sovereign, and in still other cases, both. Catholic writers express themselves to the same effect.14 Depending on the circumstances and in the strength of his dual sovereignty the pope has been able to make use of the best of two worlds.

The anomaly and riddle of this duality is also reflected in American-Vatican diplomatic relations, to which we will turn in the next section.   The pope's temporal sovereignty grew out of the States of the Papacy, and he administrated these for better or worse as any other monarch. During the twentieth century, the spiritual, religious, and moral sovereignty of the Holy See has been emphasized and the State of Vatican City as only a means to that end. The significant fact remains that any diplomatic relation with the Vatican is with the Holy See—the spiritual organ of the Roman Catholic Church. It is therefore not surprising that Protestant churches in America have historically opposed sending an ambassador to Rome. Many American Roman Catholics were, and are, likewise uneasy about the same.

That the State of Vatican City functions as a means to an end for the Holy See is obvious from the administrative structure of both.   The term "Holy See" is used in three different ways:

"Sometimes...it denotes the Pope together with the central offices of the Roman Curia, formed of the sacred congregations, the tribunals and the various other departments. Sometimes it designates the Pope in his role as visible head of the Church, possessing the apostolic primacy as successor of St. Peter. Finally, it sometimes indicates the spiritual organisation of papal government."[15] Further, the Holy See "exists and operates within the international community as the juridical personification of the Church, it enjoys the right to negotiate agreements and treaties with other international subjects..., it exercises the active and passive right of legation....The Holy See's sovereignty has been recognised explicitly in many international agreements."[16]

In the central government of the Holy See the pope is supreme but he is assisted by the cardinals whom he appoints. They are addressed "Your Eminence." Until the time of John XXIII their number was limited to seventy, but since then it has more than doubled. They constitute the College of Cardinals, who elect the pope and serve as an advisory body which he may call from time to time to deal with major issues. Individually they also assist him in different ways. Only a minority of the cardinals reside in Rome, where they are assigned to specific duties or offices in the Curia.

The Roman Curia is the organ of the central administration of the Church, world wide. Local jurisdiction is exercised by the bishops, but the more than two thousand residential sees around the world are obliged to obey specific instructions of the pope.

Canon Law defines the Roman Curia in the following terms: "The Supreme Pontiff usually conducts the business of the universal Church by means of the Roman Curia, which fulfills its duty in his name and by his authority for the good and the service of the churches; it consists of the Secretariat of State or the Papal Secretariat, the Council for the Public Affairs of the Church, congregations, tribunals and other institutions, whose structure and competency are defined in special law."[17]

There are nine congregations—in terms of a secular government comparable to ministries—which deal administratively with such aspects of the life of the church as the bishops, Catholic education, the clergy, doctrine of the Faith, Oriental churches, propagation of the Faith, religious and secular institutions, sacraments and divine worship and causes of saints. Each of these entities consists of cardinals and bishops with a staff. The congregation is chaired by a prefect, who is generally a cardinal.

In addition to these administrative entities are found three tribunals which have "legal" jurisdiction, as in matters of conscience and second marriage, and serve as courts of appeal. There are other administrative offices having responsibility in the areas of finance, the maintenance and operation of the household of the pope, and commissions carrying out various tasks, often of a temporary nature.

John XXIII and Paul VI initiated the establishment of three permanent secretariats. The first is for promoting the unity of Christians, the second has as its objective to develop relationships with non-Christian believers, and the third seeks to dialogue with atheists and study the reason for religious indifference.

Last but foremost, the Holy See includes the Secretariat of State and the Council for Public Affairs of the church. The latter was previously a part of the Secretariat of State, but was organized by Paul VI as an agency to oversee diplomatic relations with governments that have ambassadors accredited to the Holy See. The Secretary of State is the head of this council.

The Secretariat of State has been defined as "the chief middle manager in the Curia" and is "responsible for aiding the pope in his relationships with the universal Church and in dealing with the other departments of the Roman Curia. It is responsible for coordinating the work of the various curial offices, and regular meetings of the heads of the dicasteries are presided over by the Secretary of State." Further, "matters not clearly within the competence of one or another dicastery are handled by the Secretariat. In principle, direct access to the pope himself is through the Secretariat."[18] Accordingly, the Secretariat of State is the central organ of the Curia. The secretary who is he head of the Secretariat is now always a cardinal. He is called "Cardinal Secretary of State" and as such the chief administrative officer of the Holy See. His role has been described as that of a foreign minister and prime minister and "by all odds the secretary of state is the most conspicuous and most familiar personage at the Vatican, after the pope himself."[19]

Prior to 1870, when the popes governed the States of the Church, the Secretary of State was occupied primarily with political and economic issues. Here again is revealed what we have referred to as the riddle of Roman Catholicism. What we have in mind is expressed in these words:

> As long as the Roman Pontiffs were lords of the papal states, political questions absorbed much of the attention of the cardinal secretary. There was not one secretary for political affairs and another for ecclesiastical matters. From the viewpoint of the modern mind a division of competences would seem appropriate and even necessary. From the Roman viewpoint, however, the separation was impractical. The two roles could not be separated in the Pope's first minister any more than they could be separated in the Pope himself.[20]

After 1870 the Secretary of State was occupied with the administration of the Holy See, but retained the title even though there was no state. After 1929 his main responsibilities are found in the Holy See, while at the same time he oversees the small Vatican State. However, the ambassadors are accredited to the Holy See, and the Secretary of State is in charge of the agencies dealing with papal diplomacy because he is in charge of the Holy See, and not because he oversees those who administrate the city-state. Yet, since he bears the title Secretary of State it has appeared to some that the ambassadors are accredited to the State and not to the Holy See, the supreme administrative organ of the church. In the commentary on the Roman Curia the editors of the Code of Canon Law came closer to a true description of the title when they wrote: "Secretariat of State or Papal Secretariat."[21]   It seems the latter would be the only appropriate designation.

One of the most important responsibilities of the Secretary of State is the supervision of the papal legates and papal diplomatic activities around the world. There are three functions of the legates, and thus three types of legates: (1) The apostolic or pontifical legates who represent the pope to the churches in a certain country "so that day by day the bonds of unity which exist between the Apostolic See and particular churches become stronger and more efficacious." (2) The papal representative (ambassador) to a nation that has diplomatic relations with the Holy See, with the title Nuncio or Pro Nuncio, depending upon whether he is the dean of the diplomatic corps. In most cases the same person is also apostolic legate, reflecting the fact that he has the religious responsibility of a papal nuncio as well as the rank and function of ambassador. When an apostolic legate is not a nuncio because the country in which he resides has no ambassador at the Holy See, he still assists the church in dealing with the government in behalf of the country. (3) The pope's representative at various international organizations or conferences.22

THE MISSION OF THE CHURCH:
The Reason for Diplomatic Activities

The objective of papal diplomatic relations is to gain favor for the Roman Catholic Church and to assure the free exercise of its mission and its ecclesiastical prerogatives, which include control of church property, and that its teachings on education, marriage, and family life be respected (and if possible supported) by the civil government. Usually the object of a concordat concluded with a certain nation is to obtain preferential treatment. Our purpose in clarifying the organizational structure of the Holy See and papal diplomatic activity is to point out that any diplomatic relation with the Vatican, in whatever form, is with the Holy See and thus to establish a unique relationship between the Roman Catholic Church and the nations of the world and major international organizations.

The motivation and justification for papal diplomacy is the church's mission specifically entrusted to it by Christ as expressed in these words:

The fundamental title or right that the Apostolic Holy See must exercise in the international community arises from a prerogative of temporal independence juridically recognized and guaranteed, and is none other than the religious power or authority of the

Supreme Pastor of the Catholic Church—to be sure,
not just that religious and pastoral power considered
in itself but also in the historical, social and temporal
radiance of the religious and pastoral power.23

Monsignor Mario Oliveri, serving at the Apostolic Delega-
tion in London, writes in the same vein:

With regard to the Political Community, the functions of Pontifical Representatives cannot be defined
as a political activity. Their functions are essentially
religious in character and find their context in the activities of the Holy See ad extra in its service of the
Churches and of the World.   The activities of
Pontifical Representatives also bear witness in this
sphere to the fact that the Church, while primarily
and essentially concerned with the establishment of
God's Kingdom in the World, cannot on this account
overlook any aspects of men's lives.24

The primary source for diplomatic missions of the church is
found in the pope, who, as the successor of Peter and Vicar of
Christ, possesses spiritual, religious, and moral sovereignty. Gino
Paro writes: "The Holy See claims recognition as a juridical personality in the international community, basing this claim both on
tradition and on the very nature of its mission in the world. A logical consequence of this status is the exercise of the right of diplomatic legation, in as much as this is essential for participation in international affairs." Paro then asks "whether the Papal practice of
sending diplomatic agents is founded simply on the concessions of
certain States, or on international courtesy." He answers, "Evidently
the foundation of the right of papal legation is something deeper than
custom. Since this right is based on the primacy of the Roman
Pontiff it is clear that it is intimately bound up with the constitution
of the Church." In his conclusion he states categorically: "The
exercise of the right of legation is a manifestation of participation in
international life, and for this reason alone it is due to the Holy See.
Nevertheless the right of papal legation is based on theological and
juridical principles which transcend international law: its foundation

is the primacy of the Pope."25   Robert A. Graham reaches a similar conclusion:

> Freedom of conscience implies freedom to organize religious life in the form consistent with one's belief. If the citizen recognizes the Pope of Rome as such a guide, the State has no choice but to bow and to make its calculations on that basis. It may be added that when such international organs as the World Council of Churches assume a comparable role of authoritative guide, the State will in all consistency need to take that into account. In the meantime, the civil power is not acting in a discriminating fashion when it accredits its diplomatic representatives to the only religious authority which affords peremptory guidance to consciences.26

To the question, Would an appointment of an ambassador to the Holy See imply recognition of the pope as such?   James J. Hennesey, S.J., replied:

> If there were to be an American Ambassador to the Vatican, he would have to be ambassador to the Pope as Pope. This would not demand United States recognition of all the Papal claims implied in the titles "Vicar of Jesus Christ, Successor to the Prince of the Apostles, Supreme Pontiff of the Universal Church," but, to speak realistically, it would mean that the United States acknowledged the fact that such claims were made, and that a reality existed to substantiate them, and that the importance of that reality, the spiritual authority of the Pope, was such that it warranted establishment of diplomatic relations.27

The influence, responsibility, and superiority of the religious order over the temporal was expressed by John XXIII when he convoked Vatican II: "This supernatural order must, however, reflect its efficiency in the other order, the temporal one, which on so many occasions is unfortunately ultimately the only one that occupies and worries man." The pope continues by saying that in the temporal order "the Church also has shown that it wishes to be *Mater et Magistra*—Mother and Teacher—according to the words of our distant and glorious predecessor, Innocent III, spoken on the occasion of the Fourth Lateran Council."28

It should be noticed that Pope John XXIII makes reference to Innocent III and the Fourth Lateran Council in 1215, which is said to mark "the zenith of the papal theocracy."29 We have already observed that during Innocent's pontificate the papal claim of spiritual and temporal supremacy reached its highest realization, and that he was the first to name the pope "vicar of Christ, yea of God himself. Not only is he intrusted with the dominion of the Church, but also with the rule of the whole world."30 Having pointed to Innocent III as an example, John XXIII speaks further about the responsibility of the spiritual order toward the temporal society saying that "the living presence of the Church extends, by right and by fact, to the international organizations, and to the working out of its social doctrine regarding the family, education, civil society, and all related problems." Consequently, this has raised the church's "magisterium to a very high level as the most authoritative voice, interpreter and affirmer of the moral order, and champion of the rights and duties of all human beings and of all political communities."31

Cardinal Pappalardo, Archbishop of Palermo, expressed the same concept: "Since the Church should be and wants to be represented in the World, to share its hopes and sorrows and to exercise, hopefully, a beneficial influence on its diverse social and political elements, the Pontifical Representation is seen as an active instrument in the plan of the International Community and of its various organisms."32

It would not be presumptuous to conclude that the papal diplomacy has as its ultimate goal creation of the theocracy of Augustine's City of God, and that it is believed this can be realized if the voice of the Vicar of Christ with his authoritative and infallible spiritual, religious, and moral message is not only heard but also followed.

AMERICAN-VATICAN DIPLOMATIC RELATIONS

The earliest "diplomatic" or "consular" relationship between the Papal States and North America goes back to the latter part of the eighteenth century. At that time the Papal States covered a considerable part of Italy, including several Mediterranean ports. In 1784 the papal nuncio in Paris told the American chargé d'affairs that the Papal States were willing to open their ports to American ships. America responded positively and thus began her consular representation to the Papal States.

The motivation for this new relation was political and commercial, as expressed by President James K. Polk (1845-1849): "The interesting political events now in progress in these States, as well as a just regard to our commercial interests, have, in my opinion, rendered such a measure expedient."[33] It was made abundantly clear that the relation was with the Papal States and the pope as a secular ruler, not a spiritual leader of a church. The first chargé d' affaires was given the following detailed instruction:

> There is one consideration which you ought always to keep in view in your intercourse with the papal authorities. Most, if not all, the governments which have diplomatic relations at Rome are connected with the Pope as head of the Catholic Church. In this respect the government of the United States occupies an entirely different position. It possesses no power whatever over the question of religion. All denominations of Christians stand on the same footing in this country, and every man enjoys the inestimable right of worshipping his God according to the dictates of his own conscience. Your efforts therefore will be devoted exclusively to the cultivation of the most friendly civil relations with the Papal government, and to the extension of commerce between the two countries. You will carefully avoid even the appearance of interfering in ecclesiastical questions, whether these relate to the United States or any other portion of the world. It might be proper, should you

deem it advisable, to make these views known on some suitable occasion, to the papal government, so that there may be no mistake or misunderstanding on this subject.34

In the Italian civil wars the Vatican lost territory and seaports and declined politically and economically in importance. By 1867, when America closed its diplomatic mission, the Papal States had been reduced to Rome itself, which was annexed to Italy three years later, and the Papal States ceased to exist.

From 1867 to the beginning of the Second World War there was no direct diplomatic relation between the United States and the Vatican. In 1939 President Franklin D. Roosevelt appointed Myron C. Taylor as his personal representative to Pope Pius XII with the rank, but not the status, of ambassador. The ambiguity of this arrangement has been pointed out:

> Neither President Roosevelt nor his representative communicated to the Vatican, certainly not publicly, any of the denials communicated to the American public concerning the diplomatic status of the mission. Abroad it was generally recognized that the newly invented formula of "personal representative" with the rank of ambassador was only one more device employed by the young Republic in the New World to get around constitutional difficulties that the Old World had difficulty understanding. Outside the United States, Mr. Taylor was regarded for all practical intents and purposes as the diplomatic representative of the United States.35

Myron C. Taylor also served as President Truman's personal representative until he retired in 1949, at which time this ten-year United States-Vatican interim relationship came to an end. In 1951 President Truman took a further step by nominating General Mark W. Clark to be an American ambassador to the Vatican. General Clark, on account of strong public opposition, requested that the nomination be withdrawn, and accordingly it was never brought to the Senate and no diplomatic relationship was established.   President Eisenhower appointed no envoy to the Vatican, nor did Presidents Kennedy or Johnson.

In 1970 President Nixon asked Henry Cabot Lodge to make periodic visits to the Vatican for the purpose of exchanging views on international and humanitarian topics, but he did so without diplomatic status.

In the light of this brief historical survey it becomes obvious that it was a historical event when the Senate, on September 22, 1983, voted to repeal the 1867 ban on diplomatic relations with the Vatican, thus opening the way for President Reagan to appoint William A. Wilson as the first ambassador, not to the State of Vatican City re-established in 1929, but to the Holy See itself. This new relationship is significant not only in itself, but also as an indication of a shift in ideology and public opinion and policy, especially in the area of the American doctrine of separation of church and state.

When, in the past, the question of diplomatic relations came up it was always strongly opposed by political and religious organizations, but in the case of William A. Wilson the opposition came mainly from the latter. The religious opposition included the National Council of Churches, the National Association of Evangelicals, the Baptist Joint Committee on Public Affairs, Jerry Falwell for the Moral Majority, the American Jewish Congress, and other groups and individuals. Many Roman Catholics opposed the appointment and still more were uncertain.

The basic reasons for this opposition were expressed by B. B. Beach before the Judiciary Committee of the House of Representatives, on behalf of Seventh-day Adventists. He first pointed out that this "radical change in long-standing national policy was accomplished without public discussion or hearings and without substantive debate in either House. It thus seems to have circumvented the democratic process, and this gives cause for concern. The issue has been controversial and divisive, and, whenever raised, it has produced strong reactions."36 He then lists five reasons for not having an American ambassador at the Vatican: (1) the separation of church and state; (2) it is a form of religious discrimination; (3) Pope and Curia comprise the Holy See, making the ambassador an American representative to the head of the Roman

Catholic Church; (4) official diplomatic relations are unnecessary; and (5) possible damage to inter-church relations.

B. B. Beach pointed out in the closing paragraph of his report that the opposition to United States diplomatic recognition of the Holy See was not based on anti-Catholic bigotry: "No one can deny the current Pope's efforts to promote peace and his speeches supporting human rights. These endeavors are not in question. The Pope's status as a significant international figure is not the issue. The basic problem is the First Amendment to the United States Constitution and diplomatic relations with a church."[37]

Statements such as the following were, and are, common in justifying the appointment: It is for our own foreign policy interest; Vatican influence on international opinion; Pope John Paul II and President Reagan are the two world leaders who fight communism, and an ambassador brings them closer together; they, too, have a mutual concern for the problems of Central America; the pope has emerged as a political and religious world leader; the pope's popularity as the great statesman of the world today.

In its defense of the government's right to have an ambassador with the Holy See the Justice Department argues that, "An entity need only have an internationally recognized juridical personality for nations to carry on diplomatic relations with it."[38]

Archbishop Pio Laghi, the Apostolic Legate and nuncio to the United States, had pointed out "that the Holy See's authority is spiritual and moral, and is not dependent on temporal power." This fact was used by opponents, but to this the Justice Department responded by saying that "whatever the source of the authority of the Holy See, or the view of the Holy See as to the source of its world influence, that source is irrelevant. The fact is that, however the Holy See views itself, it is a highly influential player on the stage of world diplomacy." The Justice Department further declared that "The First Amendment does not require the President to ignore diplomatic realities in order to avoid contact with an internationally recognized entity that views its part in world affairs as primarily religious."[39]

The Justice Department ignored the religious aspect of the Holy See and the pope and based its assumptions entirely on political and pragmatic reasons, "To the extent that the views of the Holy

See command respect and attention on the world scene, it is imperative that the positions and interests of the United States be communicated and understood before the views of the Holy See are formulated and aired to the world."40 Further, "the mere fact that the foreign policy interests of the United States might in some cases coincide with the religious interests the Holy See represents is not in itself sufficient to violate the establishment clause."41

Senator Richard G. Lugar, who sponsored the amendment to repeal the law of 1867, praised Pope John Paul II for having made the Vatican a "significant political force for decency in the world."42

There is a new and added dimension in the arguments and reasons why an American ambassador should be appointed to the Holy See, indicating a shift in the thinking of the relationship between church and state, the spiritual and the secular and religion and politics in its various forms, nationally and internationally. We refer to the quest for a new moral order. Wilson said that his position as an ambassador had developed "from a 'listening post' mentality to a quest for morality....In these latter days, we have consciously entered into a quest to recognize and to understand the role of religion in international affairs." From the White House it was reported that President Reagan stated that "no lasting good is possible in the public sphere without spiritual renewal. The strongest voice for that renewal at the present time is that of John Paul II, the Roman Catholic Pope."43

Archbishop Pio Laghi has been constant in his statements regarding a common aspect of U.S.-Vatican relations, "for understanding the role of religion and moral principles in international affairs," as well as the pope's leadership in this goal. "In the past the Apostolic Delegate or the Papal Nuncio was often seen as a judge or a mediator of potential disputes. Today he is seen more as a witness to the authority of and role of Peter and, at the same time, to the dynamic interchange of collegial fraternity which is shared by the bishops throughout the world."44

William A. Wilson's appointment as ambassador lasted not even two years, but reasons were personal. In behalf of the Americans United For Separation of Church and State, Robert L. Maddox, the executive director, protested, as previously, the appointment of an ambassador. However, Frank Shakespeare was nominated and appointed by the Senate. Contrary to Wilson and Pio Laghi he said that he would differentiate between the political and religious concepts of the pope's leadership.[45] He perceives his work as that of exchanging information between the Holy See and the United States government. He explained, "As a citizen, I would say that the knowledge and interests of the Holy See cover a very wide spectrum, which in many ways overlay the knowledge and interests of the United States, for example, areas such as the Philippines, and the Americas and Poland and Czechoslovakia and Eastern Europe and the Soviet Union and the Mideast and Africa."[46]

We mentioned in the beginning that the religious and spiritual aspects of Roman Catholicism on the one hand, and its possession of a sovereign state and exercise of secular power and influence on the other, was a riddle which causes theological, ecclesiological, social, and political contradiction. The appointment of a United States ambassador to the Holy See and the reasons for it and the arguments against it illustrate that riddle.

Whatever reasons used for justifying an ambassador—contradictory as they are—there is nevertheless a great ideological difference between the arrangement of the American-Vatican relationship in 1784 and the one two hundred years later in 1984. When this is perceived,together with the change of emphasis and structure within the Holy See (already noted), it becomes obvious that the United States government has gone, step by step, the way of Rome.

5

CANON LAW AND PAPAL UNIVERSAL JURISDICTION

"All law is locked within my breast."[1] These words of Pope Boniface VIII (1294-1303) express the highest claim of papal authority and power. They are the culmination of a thousand years of civil and ecclesiastical lawgiving in favor of the bishop of Rome. What were the developments that prepared the way for utterance and acceptance of this lofty claim? How did canon law—the law of the church—find its principles reflected in civil law—the law of the state—and its rules enforced by the political power of the state, even by the armies of the empire? And with what effect on both church and state was this union of purpose accompanied? What influence does papal primacy and ecclesiastical jurisdiction have on civil jurisprudence and temporal and spiritual affairs in the life of the church? These questions we shall attempt to answer in exploring further the emergence of the papacy as a religious and political power.

EMPEROR CONSTANTINE AND ECCLESIASTICAL LAWS

The man who started the church up the ladder toward Pope Boniface's lofty claim was Constantine, a Roman emperor of the fourth century. His own Christian convictions subject to severe question, Constantine sought to weave the church "into the texture of the Roman Empire as a dominant element and a political bond. By this policy, he reached a success which went far beyond everything he could have hoped."[2] His interest in the church was not for the sake of the gospel or the saving of souls, but for the sake of the empire. By uniting the various religious interests through ecclesiastical laws issued by the state, and thus having the enforcement of secular power, he sought to strengthen his reign.

Given equal rights with the old religions by the Edict of Toleration in A.D. 311, Christianity gradually assumed a favored status as, through his laws, Constantine showed his favor to the Christian clergy and church. In Constantine's mind Christianity was the bond that could cement divisive elements of the empire. The empire "had one Emperor, one law, and one citizenship for all free men. It should have one religion."3

Through ecclesiastical lawgiving Constantine sought to glue together his vast empire. He issued his decree that Sunday—the day which Mithraism had dedicated to the sun—should be the official holiday. Church and state signalized their union by their official patronage of the legalized Sunday. Decisive authority under the new conditions was the emperor. "Councils of the church passed upon questions of creed and of organization, but it remained with the imperial authorities to confirm and execute the anathemas against recurring heresy or the decisions as to conflicting claims of power and precedence. For good or for evil the church was in politics."4

Great as were the favors that Constantine showed to the church, "they were only for that strong, close-knit, hierarchically organized portion that called itself the 'Catholic.' The various 'heretical' sects, and they were still many, could look for no bounty from his hands."5 In other words, the imperial state church, built upon the decrees of the state, became a persecuting and intolerant church.

THE CANONS OF CHURCH COUNCILS

Constantine had hoped that Christianity would be the glue to bind together his vast empire, but he found the unity of the church seriously threatened by the Donatist schism in North Africa. The Donatists opposed the influence of the bishop of Rome and denied the validity of ordination performed by a certain bishop who had betrayed the church during the time of persecution. They aimed at a "holy" and "pure" church. In order to settle the controversy the emperor summoned a council to meet in A.D. 314, at Arles, in present-day France. Here the Donatist contentions were condemned and, among other things, the Roman date of Easter approved. When the council met, Constantine could truly say, "I have assembled a great number of bishops from different and almost innumerable parts of the empire."6 The Council of Arles began a new era of church and state relationships. As protector of the church, Constantine claimed a measure of supervision over its internal affairs.

The Council of Nicaea, in A.D. 325, illustrates the policy of Constantine in dealing with the church. Its main work was the condemnation of Arianism, which taught a distorted view of the nature of Christ, but the council also decreed twenty canons.7 Canons four, five, and six are of special interest in an evaluation of the position of the See of Rome. Canon four legislates the appointment of bishops: "The bishop shall be appointed by all (the bishops) of the eparchy (province)." Then "the confirmation of what is done belongs by right, in each eparchy, to the metropolitan." Canon five deals with excommunication. "The sentence passed by the bishops of each province shall have the force of law, in conformity with the canon which says: He who has been excommunicated by some shall not be admitted by others." Canon six begins: "The old customs in use in Egypt, in Libya, and in Pentapolis,...shall have jurisdiction over all these (provinces); for there is a similar relation for the Bishop of Rome. The rights which they formerly possessed must also be preserved to the Churches of Antioch and to the other eparchies."

These canons, issued by the first general council, do not speak about the supremacy of the bishop of Rome. The bishop of Rome had the same right in his province as the other bishops in their provinces, and had no jurisdiction outside his own province.

Between the first general council at Nicaea in A.D. 325 and the second general council at Constantinople in A.D. 381, the question of the deity of Christ divided the churches in the East and in the West. An arrangement was made between Constantine's two sons, Constantius and Constans, that a council should be held at Sardica in A.D. 343, to see if peace could be restored between the church of the East and the church of the West. It was planned to be a new general council, but the Eastern bishops, finding themselves outnumbered by those of the West, withdrew, and instead of bringing the two groups together another rift was created.8 The council failed in the main purpose for which it was called, but was of great importance in the development of the judicial power of the bishop of Rome.9

Canons three and five are, in this connection, of special interest. The content of these two canons as well as of canon four is summarized by Charles Y. Hefele in the following way: "When a bishop has been deposed by his comprovincials at the Provincial Synod, but still thinks his cause a good one, he may, according to the fifth canon, either appeal to Rome himself, or through the judges of the first court....In case a bishop deposed by the first court appeals to Rome, his See may not be given to another until Rome has decided, that is, has either confirmed the sentence of the first court, or appointed a court of appeal."10

The Roman Catholic Church often refers to these two canons, but it should be noticed that "Sardica" was only a Western council, and as such could not decree anything which would affect the churches outside the territory of the bishop of Rome. The other churches had withdrawn from the council. The two Western emperors, Gratian and Valentinian II, issued a decree (A.D. 378) which gave full support to Roman jurisdiction. The decree stated that if "the offender himself is a metropolitan, then perforce he shall go without delay to Rome or to such men as the Roman bishop appoints as judges,... And if a metropolitan bishop or any other prelate is suspected of partiality or prejudice, the accused may appeal to the bishop of Rome or to a council of fifteen bishops of the vicinity."11

Emperor Theodosius (A.D. 379-395) in the East gave full support to the Nicene Creed and therefore endorsed the orthodoxy of the bishop of Rome when he wrote it was his "will that all the peoples subject to the government of our clemency shall follow that religion which the holy Peter delivered to the Romans, as pious tradition from him to the present times declares it, and as the pontiff Damasus manifestly observes it."12 Only those who follow the teaching of Rome should "be included under the name of catholic Christians. All others we pronounce mad and insane and require that they bear the ignomiy of teachers of heresy."13

It is significant that the emperors issued these decrees, not a church assembly. In evaluating these decrees and the decision at Sardica it is necessary to balance them with the second general council at Constantinople in A.D. 381. The interesting facts are that Theodosius called the council, the bishop of Rome was not present—nor was he even represented—yet it ultimately gained repute as the second general council. The various and contradictory decisions, which had been made at the many synods or local councils during the time between the two general councils, had permanent value only if they were in harmony with the decisions of the Council of Constantinople. This council, which was called by Emperor Theodosius, made null previous statements regarding a universal Roman jurisdiction as is evident from canon two, which also gave a blow to the decision of Sardica. The second canon reads as follows:

> The bishops are not to go beyond their dioceses to churches lying outside of their bounds, nor bring confusion on churches; but let the bishop of Alexandria, according to the canons, alone administer the affairs of Egypt; and let the bishops of the East manage the East alone,…which are mentioned in the canons of Nicaea, being preserved; and let the bishops of the Asian diocese administer the Asian affairs only; and the Pontic bishops only Pontic matters; and the Thracian bishops only Thracian matters. And let not the bishops go beyond their dioceses for ordination or any other ecclesiastical ministrations, unless they be invited.[14]

The third canon stated that the "bishop of Constantinople, however, shall have the prerogative of honor after the bishop of Rome; because Constantinople is New Rome."[15] It should be noticed that it was one of honor only—as the capital city—not of jurisdiction.

In spite of the decisions made at the first two general councils the bishop of Rome continually pressed the claim for spiritual supremacy. Pope Innocent I, A.D. 402-417, asserted the authority of the Roman See with all dignity and pre-eminence, and the popes who succeeded him ascribed the decisions of Sardica to the Council of Nicaea, and based on them a universal jurisdiction of the bishop of Rome. Thus from the very beginning forgeries played a great part in the development of papal supremacy.

At the third general council in Ephesus, A.D. 431, we find the Pope Celestine playing a prominent part. However, it did not occur "to the emperor, or to the bishops in general, that the grave doctrinal question in dispute ought to be settled by the 'Supreme Pontiff.'"16

During the pontificate of Leo I (A.D. 440-461) we find papal decisions enforced by civil law. The bishopric of a certain Celidonius had been given to another while he was sick. Celidonius appealed to Rome and cleared himself. As punishment Leo stripped Hilary, metropolitan of Arles, "of all his rights as metropolitan, attaching his province to the see of Vienne and only allowing him to retain his own see as a special act of grace. It was an execution with the full rigour of the law."17 The absolutism of the Roman Pontiff became part of the law of the empire and he became supreme head of the Western church.

One church historian dwells on the case of Hilary "because [of] his righteous resistance to the arbitrary interference of Pope S. Leo."18 After having cited the emperor's decree he continues: "Thus did the decrepit autocracy of the dying empire plant in the home of freedom, the Church of God, the hateful likeness of itself. This rescript of Valentinian goes far beyond the rescript of Gratian. It makes the pope's word law, and it makes the bishops his humble servants."19 Certain it is that "papal *jurisdiction* outside the suburbicarian provinces mainly arose out of the legislation of the State. One may truly say Erastianism begat it, and forgery developed it."20

This development must now be compared with the enactments of the fourth general council at Chalcedon in A.D. 451. The main task of the council was to confirm the orthodox belief regarding the divine-human nature of Christ, which was done by reaffirming the Nicene Creed.

Prior to the council, Pope Leo I had written a summary of the Christian doctrine on the nature of Christ. This so-called Tome, in which the pope sets forth the view which the West had entertained since the time of Tertullian, was read at the council. This done, the bishops exclaimed: "That is the faith of the fathers, that is the faith of the apostles! We all believe thus, the orthodox believe thus! Anathema to him who believes otherwise! Peter has spoken by Leo."21

In connection with the respect shown Leo for his orthodoxy, it is interesting to notice the honor paid to the Emperor Marcian. At the sixth session the emperor and empress were present. After the declaration of faith set forth at the previous session had been read, the emperor asked if it expressed the view of all. The three hundred and fifty-five bishops answered with the exclamation:

> We all believe thus, there is one faith, one will; we are all unanimous, and have unanimously subscribed; we are all orthodox! This is the faith of the fathers, the faith of the apostles, the faith of the orthodox; this faith has saved the world. Prosperity to Marcian, the new Constantine, the new Paul, the new David! You are the peace of the world! ... Thou hast strengthened the orthodox faith! Many years to the Empress! You are the lights of the orthodox faith, by which peace everywhere prevails! Marcian is the new Constantine, Pulcheria the new Helena.22

The council's fifteenth session enacted a series of canons of which three are of special significance when evaluating the papal claim of universal jurisdiction. Canons nine and seventeen gave the bishop a right to appeal from his metropolitan to the exarch or the see of the imperial Constantinople. Rome is not mentioned. Canon twenty-eight gave Constantinople parallel jurisdiction with Rome because Constantinople was the New Rome.23

EMPEROR JUSTINIAN'S LAWGIVING

During the reign of Emperor Justinian I (A.D. 527-565) the Roman Empire was once more united, and the popes and the church, who had had a certain independence on account of the invasions of various barbarian tribes, were again subjected to the emperor. We are told that "Justinian, like Constantine, exercised the right to legislate for every phase of Church life. His theory was that 'human and divine authority,' that is civic and ecclesiastical law, 'combining in one and the same act,' formed 'one true and perfect law for all.'" Further, "He meant to exercise a spiritual power very much like the temporal power he wielded.... The jurisdiction of the clergy was clearly defined and minutely regulated as an extension of civil power."24

Justinian codified the Roman law and incorporated ecclesiastical laws in his *Corpus Juris Romani*. In this way ecclesiastical laws were enforced by civil authority. Justinian issued severe laws against heretics—that is, those who were not in harmony with the bishop of Rome. Heretics, decreed Justinian, "might not hold public office, engage in the liberal professions, hold meetings or maintain churches of their own, or even enjoy all the civil rights of the Roman citizen: for them, said Justinian, 'to exist is sufficient.'"25 In the case of Manichaeism, a heretical sect, the death penalty was decreed. The law of Justinian also decreed the death penalty on those who denied the Trinity and repeated baptism. During the Protestant Reformation the reformers used this law of Justinian to justify persecution and capital punishment of Anabaptists and Anti-Trinitarians.

The church taught Justinian's Code to the barbarian nations of Europe, and inasmuch as ecclesiastical laws were a part of the Code, the spiritual as well as the temporal power of the papacy was strengthened. Ecclesiastical laws were enforced by civil law. Central and Northern Europe were "christianized" to a large degree through the enforcement of Justinian's *Corpus Juris Romani*. The medieval church became in fact a most powerful political institution.

In the year A.D. 533 Justinian issued a most significant decree concerning papal supremacy:

> Therefore we have been diligent *both in subjecting and uniting unto your holiness all the clergy of the entire region of the East;...* and it is our firm resolve never to permit any matter touching the general state of the Church to be stirred, however manifest and free from doubt such matters may be, without noti-

fying the same to your holiness, who are *the head of
all the holy churches;* thus in all things striving to increase the honour and authority of your see.26

So sweeping an "assertion by such a powerful ruler shows
the height to which papal power had climbed by the sixth century."27 Accepting these decrees in their most literal sense, Pope
John II (A.D. 533-535) wrote: "preserving the reverence due the
Roman See, you have subjected all things unto her, and reduced all
churches to that unity which dwelleth in her alone, to whom the
Lord, through the Prince of the Apostles, did delegate   all
power;...and that the Apostolic See is in verity the head of all
churches, both the rules of the fathers and statutes of the princes do
manifestly declare, and the same is now witnessed by your imperial
piety."28   When the pope stated that the emperor had "reduced all
churches to that unity which dwelleth in her alone," and the Roman
See "is in verity the head of all churches," he expressed and defined
Roman Catholic ecumenism even of the latter part of the twentieth
century.
      The importance of Justinian's decree concerning papal
supremacy and of the time at which it was issued cannot be overem-
phasized in the history of the development of papal supremacy.
During the reign of Justinian (A.D. 527-565) the Roman Empire
was united for the last time. Shortly after his death the Lombards
entered Italy and the "popes again became more independent of the
Byzantine court.... the popes, who being the richest proprietors,
enjoyed also great political consideration in Italy, and applied their
influence to the maintenance of law and order amidst the reigning
confusion."29
      Many of the popes before Justinian's time had exercised
spiritual and temporal authority during the barbarian invasions, but it
is after the time of Justinian and beginning with the pontificate of
Pope Gregory the Great (A.D. 590-604) that the medieval papacy
begins. The church historian Philip Schaff says that Gregory the
Great, "the last of the Latin fathers and the first of the popes, connects the ancient with the medieval church, the Graeco-Roman with
the Romano-Germanic type of Christianity."30 "He was the
strongest man in Italy, and must have seemed to the Romans and to

the Lombards alike far more a real sovereign than the distant and feeble Emperor."31

The more significant result of Justinian's decree of A.D. 533 regarding papal supremacy is seen in its relation to the code of Justinian and the later canon law. It is significant that when St. Bernard criticized Pope Eugenius III (1145-1153) he said: "When, then, are we to pray? when to teach our people? when to build up the Church? when to meditate in the law? I know, of course, that the palace every day re-echoes with the sound of the laws, but they are the laws of Justinian, not those of the Lord. Is that as it ought to be? See for yourself. Surely, the law of the Lord is undefiled, converting souls."32

When the nations of Europe fought the papacy for national independence, theirs was a struggle against canon law, which was superimposed on national life. In the civil and religious opposition of the fifteenth and sixteenth centuries to canon law we find some of the beginnings of Protestantism and modern democracy. This story will be taken up later.

THE DEVELOPMENT OF CANON LAW

The origin of canon law goes back to the twenty enactments of the first general council of Nicaea, A.D. 325. To these were added decretals by bishops, canons of other church councils and enactments of Christian emperors, all of which were sources for the law of the church.

"Canon" is a Greek word for rule or measure. Thus canon law is a collection of decretals and regulations that express the norm for the life of the individual Christian as well as the church collectively. It is also designated "ecclesiastical" law.

In the sixth century Dionysius Exiguus, a monk, compiled ecclesiastical laws from different parts of the church into which he interwove decretal letters of the popes, thus implying that these had equal authority with the canons of the church councils. These papal decretals were couched in the language of imperial rescripts. Furthermore, canon law was often intermixed with Roman civil law, as Justinian's civil laws had incorporated canons of the church councils.

Early and later collections of canons and papal decretals uniformly present a picture of the pope as having exercised universal jurisdiction as well as doctrinal authority from the very beginning. His universal jurisdiction was further enhanced by the Donation of Constantine—a forgery—and the Pseudo-Isidorian Decretals, already referred to, during the renaissance under Charlemagne in the eighth and ninth centuries. The great influence of the secular ruler on ecclesiastical life during the Carolingian era tended to add a considerable amount of material to the earlier ecclesiastical laws.

Between the ninth and twelfth centuries a large number of compilations came into being. All the different collections, from diverse countries and periods, were compiled and systematized by Gratian, a monk of Bologna, sometime between 1139 and 1142. His work was entitled *Concordantia discordantium canonum,* but is known simply as the *Decretum Gratiani.* Other collections followed that of Gratian. In 1230, Pope Gregory IX made a new collection designed to replace all that had gone before. Next, Boniface VIII combined all the past decretals with his own numerous bulls into a single collection. Issued in 1298 under the name Liber Sextus it included the bull Unam Sanctam.33

The principle embodied in Unam Sanctam was the product of the canonists. Boniface's assertion that all law was locked within his breast expressed the utmost aim of papal jurisdiction and supremacy. The law was perceived to be personified in the pope and foreshadowed the Vatican Council of 1870.

With some additions and revisions, the canonical collection Liber Sextus remained the fundamental canon law until the twentieth century.   Before we turn to present-day canon law, let us note the evaluation of canon law by scholars of medieval history.

CANON LAW EVALUATED

Canon law was of immense support and help to the papacy. Each collection of papal decretals became a precedent and the basis for further claims of papal supremacy.

To a large degree the influence of canon law with its lofty claims of papal power accounts for the success of the medieval papacy. The popes themselves took the greatest interest in the development and codification of canon law. Marshall W. Baldwin, in his treatment of the organization of papal monarchy, expresses himself in the following words: "The importance of canon law to the papal revival and to the organization of the papal monarchy cannot be exaggerated. Formed in the period of restoration, often under the direction of the popes themselves, the canon law was the scientific expression of the papal power of universal jurisdiction."[34]

At large, the Protestant Reformers opposed canon law as it embodied that theology and ecclesiology of Roman Catholicism, which they sought to reform. Their attitude is symbolized in a significant act when Luther made his final break with Rome. In 1520 Luther burned, at a public event in Wittenberg, the papal bull which excommunicated him. But at the same time and into the same flames he threw a copy of canon law, which likewise burned. It has been pointed out that this act "had a deeper significance than contemporaries realized, for from that time it was to cease to be an international code. In the future the civil rulers, with few exceptions, would reserve to themselves all coercive power and refuse to act at the Church's bidding."[35] Also in 1520 Luther wrote *An Open Letter to the Christian Nobility* in which he specifically attacks papal supremacy and discredits canon law.

Looking back upon the English Reformation and the break with Rome by Henry VIII, Thomas M. Parker makes the observation that, "a committee which included Cardinal Pole, singled out as the first cause of the disorders which had provoked the Reformation and the religious crisis of the sixteenth century, the flattery of the canonists who had told Popes that their will was law. 'This', says the committee, 'is the Trojan horse out of which all abuses and dire diseases have invaded the Church.'"[36] In his study of the medieval papacy L. Elliott Binns emphasizes that "The Roman Church was the heir of the Roman people—and the Roman people, like the Greeks before them, in their political thinking aimed at conformity as the basis of stability." On account of this it would be impossible to conceive that "a number of differing forms of Christianity should exist side by side without bringing down the whole religious structure," for that "would have been to them an impossible conception." Having made these observations Binns refers to the importance of canon law and the pope as the head of a unified society:

Hence there was an emphasis on the importance of unity, which under the increasing prestige of Rome and the growth of the Canon Law tended to become uniformity. The individual lost his value at the expense of the institution, an unfortunate consequence, for from it there is only a short step to regarding power as more important than justice, to a general policy of subordinating means to ends....Thus the Papacy had before it the ideal of Christendom as a single community united in a visible head, and like the Roman state regarded its problems from the standpoint of society.[37]

The past conflict between Roman Catholic canon law and civil law and jurisdiction remains with us today. In whatever form the issues may appear—theological, ecclesiological, sociological, ethical, judicial—the basic fact remains that canon law was, as already noticed, "the scientific expression of the papal power of universal jurisdiction."[38]

PAPAL POWER AND THE CANON LAW OF 1917

On March 19, 1904, Pope Pius X announced a complete overhaul of canon law and established a commission to accomplish this task which was to work under his guidance. The result was a new collection of canon laws and decretals, the *Codex Juris Canonici,* promulgated under the aegis of Pope Benedict XV in 1917, which went into effect the following year. It is comprised of 2414 canons growing out of the church's many centuries of legal history.

The 1917 code of canon law promulgates the doctrine of the pope in four short canons (218-221). The pope is said to possess "not only an honorary primacy, but supreme and full power of jurisdiction in the whole Church concerning matters of faith and morals as well as of discipline and government" (Canon 218). At the moment of his election, the pope "obtains by divine right full power of supreme jurisdiction" (Canon 219). In his commentary on the 1917 code of canon law Charles Augustine, a Roman Catholic professor in canon law, makes the following observation on canons 218 to 221. The pontifical primacy of jurisdiction "means not only inspection or direction, but legislative, judiciary, and executive power." It is a supreme power "because it is not derived from human authority, but is of divine origin, independent of any one in the same category." The pope's plentitude of power "comprises all and every power needed for the attainment of the end for which the Church was founded," for it is "immediate" and accrued to the pope "from Christ's promise and actual bestowal." It is obtained by divine right, "*uire divino*," and in order to signify the source of papal power and primacy the pope bears the titles *Vicarius Dei* or *Vicarius Christi*.39

In his comments on the origin of papal power H. A. Ayrinhac, professor of moral theology and canon law, writes that "by virtue of the promise made to St. Peter, Christ bestows upon him [the pope] supreme jurisdiction in the Church. He does not receive it from his electors but from God Himself, and consequently no human power can set any limits to it or take it away from him."40

While Christ is the original source of divine law, the pope is "endowed with the supreme and ordinary power of enacting laws for the universal church."41 Further, "The Pope has coercive power over and in the whole Church, and may abrogate, modify, and circumscribe penal laws."42 The authority of a general council rests in the pope. Canon 228 reads: "Conciliary decrees have no obligatory force unless they are ratified by the Roman Pontiff and promulgated by his command." Further, "From the judgment of the Roman Pontiff no appeal is admissible to a general council." It is the pope alone who summons and dissolves a general council (Canon 222).43

PAPAL POWER AND THE CANON LAW OF 1983

When, in 1959, Pope John XXIII announced his plan to summon the second Vatican Council, he also made known that he intended to establish a commission to revise the 1917 code of canon law in order to update it with the decrees to be promulgated by the forthcoming council. The pontifical commission began its work just prior to his death in 1963. Twenty years later, on January 25,

1983, Pope John Paul II made an official declaration regarding acceptance of the new and revised code of canon law. The canon law of 1983 sought to bring the legislation of the church into conformity with the spirit, goals, and objectives of Vatican Council II. The changes are reflected in the fact that the code of 1983 has only 1752 canons as compared with the 2414 of the 1917 canon law.

For the purpose of the present study it is sufficient to state that no Roman Catholic doctrine has been altered; likewise, the definition of papal supremacy remains the same even though it is framed within a certain "collegiality" with the body of bishops. Before we discuss the latter we will take note of canons 331 and 333 dealing with the Roman Pontiff. They confirm Vatican I and the code of 1917. The pope is "the head of the college of bishops, the Vicar of Christ, and Pastor of the universal Church on earth;... He enjoys supreme, full, immediate and universal ordinary power in the Church, which he can always freely exercise." In the exercise of primacy the pope possesses "power over all particular churches and groupings of churches." Further, "there is neither appeal nor recourse against a decision or decree of the Roman Pontiff."[44]

A great number of canons dealing with ecclesiastical activities confirm the papal primacy by pointing out the necessary obedience to the pope and his approval. Pontifical decrees cannot be challenged (Canon 1732), neither can an act or document be reviewed if it is confirmed by the pope (Canon 1405). Categorically, it is stated, "No one can judge the First See" (Canon 1404), and the Roman Pontiff is the "supreme judge for the entire Catholic world" (Canon 1442).[45]

PAPAL POWER AND COLLEGIALITY

The introductory canon (330) to those on the Roman Pontiff reads: "Just as, by the Lord's decision, Saint Peter and the other Apostles constitute one college, so in a similar way the Roman Pontiff, successor of Peter, and the bishops, successors of the Apostles, are joined together."[46] This canon leads to the question, What is the relationship between the pope and the bishops as they are joined together in one college? The words "body" and "order" are used for the same.

Reflecting the hope that Vatican II would amend the one-sided view of Vatican I on power and authority in the church, many thought that episcopal collegiality should have been the central theme or the heart of Vatican II. This indicates the present tension within the Roman Catholic Church, among both clergy and lay people, regarding authority.

Canons 331 and 333, to which reference has been made, grew out of the document *Dogmatic Constitution on the Church* of Vatican II. In the treatment of the hierarchical structure of the church the topic was considered a continuation or clarification, but also a confirmation of Vatican I. For the sake of the unity of the episcopate Christ "placed blessed Peter over the other apostles, and instituted in him a permanent and visible source and foundation of unity of faith and fellowship." No doubt with reference to Vatican I and the ever-recurring discussion of primacy and infallibility, the statement continues with these words: "And all this teaching about the institution, the perpetuity, the force and reason for the sacred primacy of the Roman Pontiff and his infallible teaching authority, this sacred Synod again proposes to be firmly believed by all the faithful."[47]

Having firmly confirmed the Petrine theory, the document takes up the question of episcopal authority: "Continuing in the same task of clarification begun by Vatican I, this Council has decided to declare and proclaim before all men its teaching concerning bishops, the successors of the apostles, who together with the successor of Peter, the Vicar of Christ...govern the house of the living God."[48] The ministry of the bishops is dealt with next in Section 22 of the document, beginning with the statement that later became Canon 330. Here it appears that there are two sources of authority: Christ to Peter and his successor the pope, and Christ to the apostles and their successors the bishops. These two avenues of authority were then joined together in the one college or body to become the supreme authority in the church. Many wanted the document to affirm parallel power and authority, but such was not to be. The concept of collegiality (the collegiality of the pope and the bishops) is defined as follows:

> But the college or body of bishops has no authority
> unless it is simultaneously conceived of in terms of
> its head, the Roman Pontiff, Peter's successor, and
> without any lessening of his power or primacy over
> all, pastors as well as the general faithful. For in
> virtue of his office, that is, as Vicar of Christ and
> pastor of the whole Church, the Roman Pontiff has
> full, supreme, and universal power over the Church.
> And he can always exercise this power freely.[49]

This statement reminds us of Canon 331 which has already been quoted. Thus no form of collegiality can infringe upon papal supremacy as defined by Vatican I. It is only "together with its head, the Roman Pontiff, and never without this head, the episcopal order is the subject of supreme and full power over the universal Church. But this power can be exercised only with the consent of the Roman Pontiff."[50]

The supreme authority of the one college, body, or order we are discussing is exercised "in a solemn way through an ecumenical council," but "a council is never ecumenical unless it is confirmed or at least accepted as such by the successor of Peter. It is the prerogative of the Roman Pontiff to convoke these councils, to preside over them, and to confirm them."[51]

The hope which progressive Catholic bishops and theologians had had regarding the establishment of a real senate of bishops was not fulfilled. The third session of Vatican II, which closed (November 21, 1964) with the promulgation of the *Dogmatic Constitution on the Church,* was therefore disappointing.

The pressure of the bishops for a more concrete arrangement was partially met at the beginning of the fourth and last session of Vatican II. It opened on September 14, 1965 and the following day Pope Paul promulgated the apostolic constitution, *Apostolica Sollicitudo* in which he laid down the principles governing a new Episcopal Synod which he had established to assist him in the governance of the Church.

In his opening statement Pope Paul acknowledged that "many bishops during the Council" had expressed a desire for a concrete program, and the opportune time had "come to finally implement a plan" in which the Catholic bishops could more effectively share in pontifical "solicitude for the universal Church." Pope Paul closes his introduction by saying: "On our own initiative and by our apostolic authority, we erect and constitute in this city of Rome a body for the universal Church, directly and immediately subject to our authority, to which we give the special name of Synod of Bishops."52

The norms which Pope Paul VI laid down for the new Episcopal Synod were incorporated in Canon Law (Canons 342-348). The new organization was not a senate but a synod "directly and immediately subject to the authority of the Roman Pontiff." In structure it was "*ad hoc*" as the pope calls the synod when he finds it advisable. He determines the place of meeting, the agenda, and the topics for discussion. It was clearly stated that "by its very nature it is the task of the Synod of Bishops to inform and give advice,"52 in order that unity between the pope and the bishops of the entire world may be close, that information and communication may be enhanced, and that doctrinal agreement may be facilitated.

The membership of the synod are elected from the national Episcopal Conferences which have from one to four representatives depending upon the size of their own membership. The names supplied have to be confirmed by the pope. In addition the pope can appoint up to fifteen per cent of the total membership. There being more than fifty Episcopal Conferences in the world, it is estimated that a given Episcopal Synod may have up to 150 representatives. At the conclusion of each Episcopal Synod the membership automatically terminates.53

The Episcopal Synod is for the bishops a new organ of communication, but what it will accomplish depends upon the attitude and wishes of the present and future popes.

By placing the pope and the bishops in stronger juxtaposition, papal power is actually being further strengthened, for it is the pope who directs collegial and synodical activities as he sees best. As previously noticed, any collegial and synodical action and promulgation requires papal assent. The formulation of collegiality in no way involves the thousands of priests and millions of lay people within the church. Vatican II maintained the monarchial structure of the church and no democratization was envisioned or intended. The

Protestant doctrine of the priesthood of believers and the democratic principle of decision-making processes moving from the people to a governing body elected by and representing the desire of the people is foreign to the Roman Catholic hierarchical system. Roman Catholic and Protestant concepts of the source of authority, power and decision-making originate from, and move toward, diametrically opposite poles. To this subject we will later return.

6

CATHOLICITY AND ECUMENISM

It may surprise Roman Catholics and many Protestants that authentic Protestantism asserts a greater claim to catholicity than the Roman Catholic Church.

The word "catholicity" conveys the meaning of universality and is practically equivalent to the word ecumenical (sometimes spelled oecumenical), which is translated from the Greek *oikumene*, "worldwide" or "the whole inhabited world." The ancient church councils were called ecumenical because they represented the church universal.

Vatican II is considered by Roman Catholics the twenty-first Ecumenical Council, since it represented the Roman Catholic Church worldwide. Christians not of the Roman Catholic faith deny Rome that right, inasmuch as it does not represent all Christendom. In this study we will observe what concepts Protestants and Roman Catholics convey by the use of the terms "catholicity" and "ecumenism."

THE CATHOLICITY OF PROTESTANTISM

To the Protestant Fathers catholicity meant faithfulness to the ancient church in life and doctrine. They also affirmed that catholicity, in order to be genuine, should be apostolic, that is, faithful to the teaching of the apostles and the practices of the New Testament church—the primitive and pure church—before the corruption of post-apostolic times. According to authentic Protestantism and the *sola Scriptura* principle, the formulation of faith (dogma), as it developed, must be identical with the apostolic formulation revealed in

Holy Scripture. It is in the succession of apostolic proclamation, or the teaching of the Word, that catholicity is preserved. In the Nicene Creed of the fourth century apostolicity is listed as one of the four marks of the church, the other three being oneness, holiness, and catholicity.

Historical Protestantism has always emphasized its faithfulness in life and doctrine to the early ancient church. Its confessions claimed catholicity inasmuch as they draw extensively from the ancient church Fathers and the early general councils. The Protestant Reformers of the sixteenth century asserted this catholicity. According to both Luther and Calvin "the church had been Christian and catholic before the papacy; therefore it could be both Christian and catholic without the papacy. In the name of such Christian catholicity they were willing to challenge Rome." Thus writes Jaroslav Pelikan. He further observes, "Recent research on the Reformation entitles us...to say that the Reformation began because the reformers were too catholic in the midst of a church that had forgotten its catholicity."[1] Luther, in his invective against the Catholic Duke Henry of Brunswick, said: "I shall prove that we have remained with the true, ancient church, yea, that we are the true, ancient church. But you have fallen from us, that is, from the ancient church, and set up a new church in opposition to the old."[2] It will now be advantageous to examine briefly the reasons why Luther came to the conviction thus expressed.

During the years between becoming a monk in 1505 and his dramatic attack on indulgences in 1517 Luther had come to a clearer understanding of the gospel. After nailing his Ninety-five Theses on the door of the castle church in Wittenberg in that year, events drove him into a struggle for his newfound faith. During the months of June and July 1519, he debated with his appointed Catholic opponent Johann Maier Eck, their main subject being the jurisdiction of the pope and the supremacy of the Roman Church.

During the debate "Luther ventured to assert that (1) the pope exercised his authority by human, not by divine, right, and was therefore not infallible,...(2) the church of Rome was not supreme over the other churches; (3) the church councils could and did err, since they were composed of erring men and did not exist by divine right; and (4) Scripture was the ultimate, divine authority in all matters pertaining to religion."3

In the midst of the battle in which Luther now was involved, he prepared three works that set forth the main outlines of his theology. The first of these, *An Open Letter to the Christian Nobility of the German Nation Concerning the Reform of the Christian Estate,* challenged the old system by emphasizing the responsibility of the laity in church affairs. The policy of the Roman Church had been to build three walls as a papal defense: "The Romanists, with great adroitness, have built three walls about them, behind which they have hitherto defended themselves in such wise that no one has been able to reform them and this has been the cause of terrible corruption throughout all Christendom."4

Luther then attacked these three walls, one by one. The first wall was the claim of the church that her authority was superior to that of the secular state. This Luther denied: "...there is really no difference between laymen and priests, princes and bishops, 'spirituals' and 'temporals,' as they call them, except that of office and work, but not of 'estate'; for they are all of the same estate, that is, they are all Christians, among whom there can be no essential difference."5

The second wall was the dogma that only the pope could determine the meaning of Scripture: "They wish to be the only Masters of the Holy Scriptures, even though in all their lives they learn nothing from them. They assume for themselves sole authority, and with insolent juggling of words they would persuade us that the pope, whether he be a bad man or a good man, cannot err in matters of faith, and yet they cannot prove a single letter of it."6

The third wall was the assertion that a reformatory council can be called by none but the pope: "The *third wall* falls of itself when the first two are torn down. For when the pope acts contrary to the Scriptures, it is our duty to stand by the Scriptures....They have no basis in Scripture for their contention that it belongs to the pope alone to call a council or confirm its actions....There is no authority in the Church save for edification."7

Luther then proceeded to lay down a program for reformatory action. In his second treatise, *A Prelude on the Babylonian Captivity of the Church,*8 he criticized the Roman sacramental system, which he believed brought the faithful into bondage to the priestly hierarchy. He asserted that, tried by Scripture, there are only two sacraments, baptism and the Lord's Supper. He also criticized the denial of the cup to the laity. In this treatise he makes a final break with Rome, for in his opposition to papal supremacy and the sacramental system he attacked the very foundation and structure of Roman Catholicism. His appeal to a general council as the highest authority was contrary to the concept of papal supremacy. Soon after completing these two works, Luther received the pope's bull, *Exsurge Domine.* In it Leo X speaks as an infallible and supreme judge, condemning twenty-one propositions selected from Luther's writings as heretical. Among these are Luther's attack on papal supremacy and the seven sacraments.

Next, Luther wrote a tract against what he called the *Execrable Bull of Antichrist,* and a third treatise, *On the Freedom of the Christian Man,* dealing with Christian living according to the gospel of Jesus Christ. Shortly after writing the three treatises he said, "Unless I am deceived, it is the whole of Christian living in a brief form."[9] A few weeks later (December 10, 1520) he burned the papal bull, and the break with Rome was now irreparable. Four months after that, at the Diet of Worms, the highest tribunal of Europe, Luther boldly declared:

> Unless I am convicted of error by the testimony of Scripture or (since I put no trust in the unsupported authority of Pope or of councils, since it is plain that they have often erred and often contradicted themselves) by manifest reasoning I stand convicted by the Scriptures to which I have appealed, and my conscience is taken captive by God's word, I cannot and will not recant anything, for to act against our conscience is neither safe for us, nor open to us. On this I take my stand. I can do no other. God help me. Amen.[10]

The conflict between the Protestant reformers and Rome grew out of the reformers' claim and adherence to catholicity, so well expressed by Jaroslav Pelikan:

Nothing so illustrates the tragic character of the
Reformation as this: the Roman church excommunicated Luther for being too serious about his catholicism, while it retained within its fellowship the
skeptics and the scoffers who did not bother to defy
its authority. In keeping with this action, Roman
Catholics ever since have displayed an astonishing
incapacity to understand the Reformation, and an
unwillingness to admit that the religious convictions
of the reformers were animated by their fidelity to
catholic ideals.[11]

Pelikan here implies that the papal claim to universal
supremacy is challenged by the question of catholicity. Indeed, both
the Orthodox Churches and the Anglican Churches challenge papal
supremacy on this basis, observing further that God has given Peter
to the church, not the church to Peter. In this they agree with the
early Church Fathers and the Conciliar Movement, the Reforming
Councils of the fourteenth and fifteenth centuries.

In his book, *Unitive Protestantism,* John T. McNeill
emphasizes the non-catholicity of Roman Catholicism. He writes:

The Reformation was a revolt, not against the principle of unity and catholicity, but against the privileged
and oppressive monarchy of Rome—an uprising not
merely of national, but of catholic feeling, against
what had become a localized and over-centralized
imperialism in Christianity, which made true
catholicity impossible....The parish was not a congregation, but an administrative unit. The governmental aspect of unity was not supported by an
adequate religious bond. The Roman Church had
substituted the idea of "Roman obedience" for the
earlier conception of catholicity expressed in a universal free communion....In the Reformation the
Christian people were taught to think, to believe, and
to sing together, and given a new vision of the high

and universal fellowship which is the church catholic.12

THE COUNTER REFORMATION
AND CATHOLICITY

The Roman Catholic reaction to the Protestant claim of catholicity may be seen in the work of the Counter Reformation. Three agencies especially contributed to its success: the Council of Trent, the Inquisition, and the Order of the Jesuits. Only the first will be dealt with here, but it should be mentioned that the Jesuits were the guiding force behind both the council and the Inquisition, which in their hands became a tool in the Catholic reaction to Protestantism.

The Council of Trent met for the first time in 1545 and held three sessions, the last ending in 1563. The council repudiated some evils that had caused scandal, but its main task was to examine and to condemn the teachings of the Protestant reformers. For that purpose it issued a great number of decrees and canons (authoritative rules of discipline or doctrine). It ranked tradition above Scripture, included the Apocrypha in the sacred canon, and declared the Vulgate of St. Jerome to be the only approved translation of Scripture. It also reaffirmed the seven sacraments. It denounced the central doctrine of the Protestant Reformers, *sola fide*—that man is justified by faith alone—and affirmed justification by faith *and* works. The council also asserted that forgiveness of sin is not by grace alone, *sola gratia*: "If any one saith, that justifying faith is nothing else but confidence in the divine mercy which remits sins for Christ's sake; or, that this confidence alone is that whereby we are justified: let him be anathema."13

Roman Catholics define catholicity as the quality of being in harmony with the teaching and practice of the church. The source for the formulation of doctrine is not only Scripture but also tradition as it has developed under the guidance, and by the confirmation, of the pope as the successor to Peter and the Vicar of Christ. *The Profession of the Tridentine Faith* requires Catholics to affirm:

I most steadfastly admit and embrace apostolic and
ecclesiastic traditions, and all other observances and
constitutions of the same Church.   I also admit the
holy Scriptures, according to that sense which our
holy mother Church has held and does hold, to
which it belongs to judge of the true sense and interpretation of the Scriptures;...and I promise and
swear true obedience to the Bishop of Rome,
successor to St. Peter, Prince of the Apostles, and
Vicar of Jesus Christ....I do, at this present, freely
profess and truly hold this true Catholic faith, without which no one can be saved....14

This formulation by the Council of Trent (1545-1563) sets
forth the dogmatic reasons for Roman Catholic opposition to the
Protestant concept of catholicity. It claims that catholicity has been
preserved by apostolic succession, meaning that the bishops by
ordination, in an unbroken chain, are the legitimate successors of
the apostles, as the pope is the successor of Peter, prince of the
apostles, who in a unique way represents Christ. Accordingly,
catholicity means faithfulness to the teaching of the Roman Catholic
Church and obedience to the Vicar of Christ, who is the custodian,
interpreter, and formulator of truth, faith, and dogma.

Trent made clear that Roman Catholicism was not going to
compromise in any way with the Reformation; on the contrary, it
demonstrated that Rome is the "counter" of the Protestant
Reformation just as Protestantism became in principle a protest
against Roman Catholicism.

ECUMENISM AND ROMAN CATHOLICISM
BEFORE VATICAN II

The beginnings of the present-day ecumenical movement go
back to joint missionary activities by Protestant churches during the
nineteenth and early twentieth centuries. A series of foreign mission conferences culminated in the World Missionary Conference at
Edinburg in 1910 presided over by John R. Mott, who became
chairman of the International Missionary Council in 1921. The

founding of the Young Men's Christian Association in 1844 and the World Student Christian Federation in 1895 were also significant, and mention should also be made of the establishment of the inter-denominational British and Foreign Bible Society (1804), the American Bible Society (1816), and other national Bible societies. Their interaction led to the formation of the World Bible Society in 1944. Together, the Bible societies have been influential in Christian mission and the ecumenical movement.

Various denominations formed international organizations such as the Presbyterian Alliance (1875), the World Methodist Convention (1881), the International Congregational Council (1891), the Baptist World Alliance (1905), and the Lutheran World Federation (1923). Inter-church concerns for Christian service, life, and faith gave birth to the 1910 Conference and later the World Council of Churches and its Commission on Life and Work. The first meeting was held in Stockholm (1925), and the second in Oxford in 1935. The World Conference on Faith and Order which met in Lausanne in 1927 and again in Edinburg in 1937, laid the foundation for the World Council of Churches which was organized in Amsterdam in 1948. Its next General Assembly was held in Evanston, Illinois in 1954, and the third in New Delhi in 1961, which was attended by 577 delegates from nearly two hundred member churches. It was most significant that during the third General Assembly the International Missionary Council and the Orthodox Church of Eastern Europe joined the World Council of Churches.

This review of historical development provides background for an inquiry into the Roman Catholic attitude toward the ecumenical movement up to the time of Vatican II. Official documents of the Roman Catholic Church during this period indicate that Rome continued to be "counter" to Protestantism, as it was during the 300 years from Trent to Vatican I. The Dogmatic Decrees of Vatican I and the Syllabus of Errors, issued by Pius IX, confirmed the tenets of the Counter Reformation. By the decree on papal infallibility Vatican I went further than Trent, and together, with the new dogma of the immaculate conception of the Virgin Mary promulgated by Pius IX, the gulf between Roman Catholicism and most major churches of Christendom widened. The documents speak for themselves.

The dogma of the immaculate conception of Mary, proclaimed in 1854, means that Mary was free from original sin. In it the pope said: "...if some should presume to think in their hearts otherwise than we have defined (which God forbid), they shall know and thoroughly understand that they are by their own judgment condemned, have made shipwreck concerning the faith, and fallen away from the unity of the Church."15

The Syllabus of Errors was issued in 1864, and while it condemned many things that Christians in general would oppose, it also repudiated doctrines and principles fundamental to Protestantism and modern democratic states. Protestantism is held to be an error.   Anathematized is the one who says that "Protestantism is only a different form of the same Christian religion, in which we may please God as well as in the Catholic Church" (Error III, 18). Related to this is the error of those who say that "the Church has not the power to define dogmatically that the religion of the Catholic Church is the only true religion" (Error V, 21). Bible societies are condemned in company with Communism and secret societies, and clerico-liberal societies (Error IV).

The Syllabus of Errors leaves little doubt as to the papal concept of church-state relationships. Those who hold the following concepts are in error: "The Church has not the power of availing herself of force, or any direct or indirect temporal power." "National churches can be established, after being withdrawn and plainly separated from the authority of the Roman Pontiff," and "The Church ought to be separated from the State, and the State from the Church" (Errors V, 24, 37; VI, 55).16 When and where the papal claim of supremacy is acknowledged it will necessarily make an impact on church-state relationships.

The acceptance of the dogma of papal infallibility by Vatican I created, as already observed, a great gulf between Roman Catholicism and the rest of Christendom. In order better to understand the anti-Protestant feelings created during the council we may refer to one of its several dramatic scenes.

In one of the council sessions the schema on modern nationalism was presented as one of the errors brought about by Protestantism. Joseph Georg Strossmayer, a former professor of canon law and now bishop, objected to this unjust charge. Referring to the schema under discussion he said, "This judgement seems to me to be consistent neither with truth nor with charity."17 Bishop Strossmayer brought to the audience's attention that modern nationalism originated in France in direct opposition to the Christian faith, which Christians hold in common. The event is vividly portrayed in the following summary:

> The greatest storm broke out on March 22, 1870, when Bishop Joseph Georg Strossmayer affirmed in the great hall of the Council that even among Protestants there were many individuals who loved Jesus. When he went on to dispute the feasibility of deciding dogmatic questions by majority rule, the majority shouted him down. Many cried out, "Lucifer! Anathema, anathema!" Others screamed, "A second Luther! Throw him out!" All the Infallibilists loudly demanded, "Down with him, down with him!"18

It has previously been noticed that Ygnaz von Döllinger was one of the vocal opponents during Vatican I. When he returned from the council he had a conversation with his archbishop, who asserted that "there was but one Church, neither new nor old." To this Döllinger replied, "But they have made a new one."19 In other words, Döllinger declared that the dogma of infallibility was one contrary to catholicity. Because of lack of catholicity the Roman Catholic Church was no longer the true catholic church; it had become a different and therefore a new church. It was for this reason that many of those who broke with Rome after Vatican I established a new church, which was faithful to catholicity and therefore correctly could be named the Old Catholic Church.

In an encyclical promulgated in 1881 Leo XIII contended that political upheavals, especially in Germany, "have followed that so-called Reformation, whose supporters and leaders have utterly opposed sacred and civil power with new doctrines."20 In another encyclical, in 1897, he denounced the Protestant Reformation as *"rebellio Lutherana,"* which "led to a complete decay of morals."21

The anti-Protestant feelings and attitudes of Vatican I continued into the twentieth century. In a 1910 encyclical Pius X denounced the reformers as "proud and rebellious men, 'enemies of the cross of Christ.'"22 Various overtures were made to Rome for participation in ecumenical gatherings such as Upsala (1918), Stockholm (1925), and Lausanne (1927), but these were officially declined. A decree was actually issued by Rome forbidding Roman Catholics to attend the Lausanne Conference, and the next year Pius XI issued the Encyclical, *The Promotion of True Religious Unity (Mortalium Animos).*

Pius XI describes Protestant ecumenism in these words: "Convinced that rarely indeed do men lack all sense of religion, they seem to draw from this reason to hope that without great difficulty it may come about that all peoples, no matter how different their religions, will stand fraternally together in the profession of a few doctrines which will serve as a kind of common foundation for the spiritual life." But the pope does not agree with these attempts. He says, "Certainly such movements as these cannot gain the approval of Catholics." He then explains:

> The work itself is promoted with such zeal that it has gained a great variety of followers and has even ensnared the minds of Catholics with the entrancing hope of attaining a union that would seem to meet the will of Holy Mother Church to whom nothing is more hallowed than the recall and the return of her wandering children to her bosom. Yet beneath the coaxing words there is concealed an error so great that it would destroy utterly the foundations of the Catholic Faith.23

It is further stressed that Rome can never be one church among many. Having pointed out how Protestants and Roman Catholics hold contrasting doctrines, it is stated: "In such great differences of opinions we do not know how a road may be paved to the unity of the Church save alone through one teaching authority, one sole law of belief and one sole faith among Christians."24

It is made crystal clear that all the doctrines of Rome are of equal significance and must be adhered to, because they have been mediated by the pope. We read: "Therefore, as many as are of Christ give, for example, to the dogma of the Immaculate Conception the same faith they give to the mystery of the August Trinity and they believe in the Incarnation of the Word no differently than they believe in the infallible teaching power of the Pope, in the sense defined by the Vatican Ecumenical Council."25

The encyclical stipulates that Rome cannot participate in ecumenical meetings and that true unity can only be obtained by a return to Rome.

> Therefore, Venerable Brethren, it is clear why the Apostolic See has never permitted its children to take part in these congresses. The unity of Christians cannot be otherwise obtained than by securing the return of the separated to the one true Church of Christ from which they once unhappily withdrew. To the one true Church of Christ, We say, that stands forth before all and that by the will of its Founder will remain forever the same as when He Himself established it for the salvation of all mankind."26

One can only remain in "the one Church of Christ" if "he acknowledges and accepts obediently the supreme authority of St. Peter and his legitimate successors." The fault of the Protestants was that they did not "obey the Roman bishop as the high shepherd of souls." The final appeal reads as follows:

> Let these separated children return to the Apostolic See established in this city which the Princes of the Apostles, Peter and Paul, consecrated with their blood, to this See, "the root and matrix of the Catholic Church," not indeed with the idea or hope that "the Church of the living God, the pillar and

ground of truth" will abandon the integrity of the faith and bear their errors, but to subject themselves to its teaching authority and rule.27

Rome was invited to participate in forming the World Council of Churches (1948), but the Holy See declined. The next year the Holy See issued an instruction restating that the only way to unity was by a return to Rome. In the encyclical *Humani generis* (1950), Pius XII warns against mistaken views, found inside and outside of the Roman Church, which throw doubt on basic Roman Catholic doctrines and lessen the distinctions between them and those of other Christian bodies.28

It is significant that in the same year, 1950, Pius XII spoke ex cathedra in the declaration of the bodily assumption of the Virgin Mary and thereby went a step further than Pius IX, who had declared the immaculate conception of the Virgin Mary. Thus the infallible teaching office of the pope was reinforced and the difference between Roman dogma and the faith of the Christian churches was still further emphasized. The declaration closes with these words:

...by the authority of our Lord Jesus Christ, of the Blessed Apostles, Peter and Paul, and by Our own authority We pronounce, declare, and define that the dogma was revealed by God, that the Immaculate Mother of God, the ever Virgin Mary, after completing her course of life upon earth, was assumed to the glory of heaven both in body and soul. Therefore, if anyone, which may God forbid, should dare either to deny this, or voluntarily call into doubt what has been defined by Us, he should realize that he has cut himself off entirely from the divine and Catholic faith.29

Notice the words Us and Our are capitalized, implying papal supremacy, and teach infallibility. The new doctrine was declared in the Holy Year of 1950, and the year 1954 was dedicated to the Virgin Mary and named "Marian year." This was the centennial year for the declaration of the immaculate conception of the Virgin Mary.

In passing we may notice that a special memorial service was held in St. Peter's on March 5, 1978, to commemorate the one-hundredth anniversary of the death of Pius IX. Attempts for beginning the procedures of his canonization had taken place, but were blocked. However, in 1985 initial steps were taken "towards possible canonization...with the official recognition of his 'heroic virtue'."30

In Rome's opposition to Protestantism there is a direct line from Trent and the Counter Reformation through Vatican I down to Pius XII, who died in 1958. With his death and the election of Pope John XXIII a new era began for the ecumenical movement. For the present study the pertinent question is, Will the new era change Roman Catholic dogma, specifically the papal claim of infallibility and universal supremacy?

ECUMENISM AND ROMAN CATHOLICISM
AFTER VATICAN II

In his opening speech on the first day of Vatican II (October 11, 1962) Pope John XXIII answered the question with which we closed the previous paragraph. Dealing with the principle duty of the Council as the defense and advancement of truth, the pope said: "The greatest concern of the Ecumenical Council is this: that the sacred deposit of Christian doctrinc should be guarded and taught more efficaciously."31 The concern of John XXIII was clearly pastoral: the "rich treasures" of the church, gathered through its long history, should be kept intact, and Vatican II would remain faithful to that heritage. He emphasized catholicity as Rome perceives it:

> Our duty is not only to guard this precious treasure, as if we were concerned only with antiquity, but to dedicate ourselves with an earnest will and without fear to that work which our era demands of us, pursuing thus the path which the Church has followed for twenty centuries. The salient point of this Council is not, therefore, a discussion of one article or another of the fundamental doctrine of the Church

which has repeatedly been taught by the Fathers and by ancient and modern theologians, and which is presumed to be well known and familiar to all.32

The key word characterizing Vatican II Council was *aggiornamento* meaning updating or renewal. The documents which resulted from the work of the council were framed with a pastoral concern in mind. In that concern the church was given a facelift, but fundamentally or doctrinally there was nothing new. The document on Ecumenism clearly expresses the desire for dialogue and action with non-Roman Catholics—this was new in itself—but at the same time it definitely warns against "a false conciliatory approach which harms the purity of Catholic doctrine and obscures its assured genuine meaning."33

In the same document a new appreciation for the Scriptures is apparent, but it should be noticed that there is a different understanding of Scriptural authority as compared with the *sola Scriptura* principle of Protestantism. We read, "But when Christians separated from us affirm the divine authority of the sacred Books, they think differently from us—different ones in different ways—about the relationship between the Scriptures and the Church. In the Church, according to Catholic belief, an authentic teaching office plays a special role in the explanation and proclamation of the written word of God."34 Thus the "authentic teaching office" of the pope is reaffirmed.

The closing paragraph of the Decree on Ecumenism contains these words:

> This most sacred Synod urges the faithful to abstain from any superficiality or imprudent zeal, for these can cause harm to true progress towards unity. Their ecumenical activity must not be other than fully and sincerely Catholic, that is, loyal to the truth we have received from the apostles and the Fathers, and in harmony with the faith which the Catholic Church has always professed, and at the same time tending toward that fullness with which our Lord wants His body to be endowed in the course of time.35

The document bearing the title *The Dogmatic Constitution on the Church,* the central one of the council, was solemnly promulgated at the close of the third session (November 21, 1964) together with the decrees on Ecumenism and Eastern Catholic Churches. By the time these three documents were promulgated John XXIII had died (June 3, 1963) and Paul VI was pontiff. Keeping in mind the confirmation of Roman catholicity by John XXIII, it is worth noticing that on the same day the three documents were promulgated Paul VI gave a speech in which he made the following comment:

> It would seem to us that the best commentary is that through this promulgation nothing in traditional doctrine is really changed. What Christ wants, we also want. That which was, remains. What the Church has taught for centuries, we likewise teach....The only difference is that what was simply lived previously is now declared expressly; what was uncertain has been clarified; what was meditated on, discussed and in part controverted now reaches a serene formulation.36

The principle stumbling block of Roman Catholicism for all non-Roman Catholics, as well as many Roman Catholics, has always been the papal claim of infallibility and supremacy. As already observed the latter was taken for granted by Vatican II, never diluted but confirmed. In his opening speech to the council (October 11, 1961) Pope John XXIII emphasized that he summoned it by virtue of being the successor of Peter, "the Prince of the Apostles who in addressing you intended to assert once again the magesterium (teaching authority) which is unfailing and perdures until the end of time."37

Rome's sacramental system, which fundamentally divides Roman Catholicism and Protestantism, was confirmed. The veneration of the Virgin Mary was further extolled by proclaiming her Mother of the Church at the close of the third session, when the decree on Ecumenism was issued. Even the casual observer will notice the increased emphasis on the Virgin Mary in Catholic worship and papal statements.

The goals of Roman Catholic ecumenism and the means by which to obtain them were outlined in Pope John's opening speech. He affirmed that the church must always oppose error but admits that "frequently, she has condemned them with greatest severity. Nowadays, however, the Spouse of Christ prefers to make use of the medicine of mercy rather than that of severity. She considers that she meets the needs of the present day by demonstrating the validity of her teaching rather than by condemnations."[38]

Pope John saw the unity of Christendom and the human family as a goal for which the Catholic Church should work. He perceived the message of unity shining forth, "as it were, with a triple ray of beneficent supernal light: namely, the unity of Catholics among themselves, which must always be kept exemplary and most firm; the unity of prayers and ardent desires with which those Christians separated from this Apostolic See aspire to be united with us; and the unity in esteem and respect for the Catholic Church which animates those who follow non-Christian religions."[39]

The *aggiornamento* of Vatican II led to the formulation of Roman Catholic ecumenism as the quest for unity of mankind within a series of concentric circles.

The inner circle is the Roman Catholic Church renewed and updated. The Roman Catholic Church itself was the central object of attention at the council. The two longest documents were the *Dogmatic Constitution on the Church* and the *Pastoral Constitution on the Church in the Modern World*. While the church itself was central in the discussions, it was not in isolation from the world as indicated in the Latin text where the initial words of the first document were "The Light of All Nations" (*Lumen gentium*), and of the second "Joy and Hope" (*Laudium et spes*). The other council documents supplement these.

Next to the Roman Catholic Church stand the Eastern Catholic Churches. Being in communion with Rome by recognizing papal supremacy they are also named the Uniate Churches. They have their own rites and canon law; they offer communion under both kinds and baptism by immersion. The clergy is permitted to marry. They are divided into a number of national groups in the

Middle East and Eastern Europe, as for example the Maronites of Lebanon (also found in Syria, Palestine, Cyprus, and Egypt), and the Uniate Church among the Copts and the Armenians. The Uniate Christians number about eight million, and approximately one million representatives are found in the United States.

The Second Vatican Council issued a *Decree on Eastern Catholic Churches* in which their unique position was re-stated. A special appeal was given to these churches to assist in their endeavor to bring the other Eastern Churches into communion with Rome. Alexander Schmenann, dean at St. Vladimir's Orthodox Seminary, Yonkers, New York, wrote a response to this special document. His opening statement reads: "It is not easy for an Orthodox to express his views on this particular Decree for the simple yet important reason that the very existence of the 'Uniate' Eastern Catholic Churches has always been considered by the Orthodox as one of the major obstacles to any sincere theological confrontation with the Roman Catholic Church."[40]

Next Alexander Schmenann points out the reason for the objection from an Orthodox point of view. First, the liturgical and canonical tradition of the East cannot be isolated from the doctrinal principles, and this is the real issue between Roman Catholicism and Eastern Orthodoxy. Secondly, the document gives the Patriarch in the Eastern Catholic Churches jurisdiction over the other bishops, but that is alien to the tradition of the Orthodox Church "where the Patriarch or any other Primate is always a *primus inter pares* [first among equals]."[41] This leads us to the third ecumenical circle: the Eastern Orthodox Churches.

The Vatican II document on ecumenism contains a declaration on *The Special Position of the Eastern Churches*. It is an urgent, even passionate, appeal for unity, closing with these words: "this sacred Synod hopes that with the removal of the wall dividing the Eastern and Western Church there may at last be but one dwelling, firmly established on the cornerstone, Christ Jesus, who will make both one."[42]

Earlier in his life Pope John XXIII had been an Apostolic Legate to Bulgaria, Rumania, Greece and Turkey, and as such, made close contacts with the Orthodox Church. His successor, Paul VI, kept up these contacts. It made news when he, early in

1964, met, embraced, and prayed with Patriarch Athenagoras of Istanbul at the Holy Sepulcher in Jerusalem. Nearly two years later, during the last days of Vatican II, a declaration was issued (December 7, 1965) simultaneously in Rome and Istanbul that the excommunication and anathemas of 1054, which led to the schism between the two churches, should be obliterated. This was followed in 1967 by a visit of Pope Paul to Istanbul and by Athenagoras to Rome.

The Orthodox Church is composed of fifteen autonomous and semi-autonomous churches and in spite of Athenagoras' relation to Rome any rapprochement to Rome is looked upon with great suspicion by many. For example, the Orthodox Church of Greece declined to send an observer to Vatican II. The doctrinal and ecclesiological differences go deep, but papal supremacy is the great stumblingblock.

The Anglican Churches are national churches but in communion with one another and have the Archbishop of Canterbury as their primate. In liturgy and ecclesiology the Anglican Church has much in common with the Orthodox Churches. The two churches have held joint doctrinal conferences. The Archbishop of Canterbury, Michael Ramsay, visited the Patriarchs of Moscow and Greece in 1962, Rumania in 1965, and Jerusalem and Belgrade in 1966.

Canterbury is also close to the Protestant churches and serves in many instances as a bridge to Roman Catholicism. It has played a strong role in the ecumenical movement and in the rapprochement with Rome. In March 1966 the Archbishop of Canterbury met with the Pope in Rome, and in a joint statement they declared that a dialogue should begin between the two churches and that to facilitate the work commissions should be set up. Personal contacts between the pope and the Archbishop of Canterbury, and the work of special commissions dealing with doctrinal and ecclesiological issues have continued. But the great issue which always surfaces is whether the pope is supreme, or a *primus inter pares*.

We suggest that the next circle is that of the Protestant churches, which Rome finds it difficult to call churches. In the document they are generally described as communities "separated from full communion with the Catholic Church—developments for which, at times, men of both sides were to blame." The decree continues by saying: "However, one cannot impute the sin of separation to those who at present are born into these Communities and are instilled therein with Christ's faith. The Catholic Church accepts them with respect and affection as brothers. For men who believe in Christ and have been properly baptized are brought into a certain, though imperfect, communion with the Catholic Church."[43]

It seems implied in the statement that all those who are baptized—even though their community is imperfect—belong unconsciously to the Catholic Church. Samuel McCrea Cavert, a former secretary of the National Council of Churches and one of the founders of the World Council of Churches, wrote a response to the Decree on Ecumenism in which he made the observation that by referring to the Protestant bodies as "ecclesial communities" it "seems to imply a modification of the traditional Catholic attitude. At least, it suggests that the corporate life of Protestants has some kind of churchly reality." However, he continues by saying: "But, on the other hand, the hesitation in speaking of non-Catholic bodies as Churches apparently implies a difference between 'Church' and 'ecclesial community.' What is this difference? Non-Catholics still need further light as to how far the Catholic Church goes in acknowledging the reality of the Church beyond its own borders."[44]

Catholic ecumenism as it relates to the Protestant churches is clearly defined by the Decree. We read:

> Nevertheless, our separated brethren, whether considered as individuals or as Communities and Churches, are not blessed with that unity which Jesus Christ wished to bestow on all those whom He has regenerated and vivified into one body and newness of life—that unity which the holy Scriptures and the revered tradition of the Church proclaim. For it is through Christ's Catholic Church alone, which is the all-embracing means of salvation, that the fullness of the means of salvation can be obtained. It was to the apostolic college alone, of which Peter is

the head, that we believe our Lord entrusted all the
blessings of the New Covenant, in order to establish
on earth the one Body of Christ into which all those
should be fully incorporated who already belong in
any way to God's People.45

Vatican II also sought to establish a new relationship with
non-Christian religions. In a Declaration issued for that purpose
reference is made to the Jews, Moslems, Hindus, and Buddhists.46
It speaks about "the spiritual bond linking the people of the New
Covenant with Abraham's stock."   Esteem is expressed for the
Moslems who like the Christians and the Jews are monotheist. "On
behalf of all mankind" an appeal is made to both Jews and Moslems
to "make common cause of safeguarding and fostering social justice,
moral values, peace, and freedom."
    The other religions tell us of man's striving to find answers
to life's meaning and they meditate on the mystery of eternal values
which may reflect divine truth. "The Church therefore has this ex-
hortation for her sons; prudently and lovingly, through dialogue and
collaboration with the followers of other religions, and in witness of
Christian faith and life, acknowledge, preserve, and promote the
spiritual and moral goods found among these men, as well as the
values in their society and culture."47
    Roman Catholic outreach includes atheists. It is firmly as-
serted that atheism is rejected in "root and branch," yet the church
should strive to detect in the atheistic mind the hidden causes for the
denial of God. Further, "the Church sincerely professes that all
men, believers and unbelievers alike, ought to work for the rightful
betterment of this world in which all alike live. Such an ideal cannot
be realized, however, apart from sincere and prudent dialogue."48
The church also "courteously invites atheists to examine the gospel
of Christ with an open mind."

Finally, the world at large is included within the spheres of
papal responsibility. It is not without significance that Pope Paul
VI, during the last session of Vatican II, flew to New York to speak
at the United Nations (October 4, 1965), appealing for world peace.
The travels and activities of Pope John Paul II are constantly making

news. Our study of Vatican diplomacy confirms the view of the church's mission for the secular world.

Any set of concentric circles has a center likewise the concentric circles of Roman Catholic ecumenism. In the center we find the pope who, being the successor of Peter, is Christ's vicar on earth and as such the centralizing power of unity for all the circles, the total mankind, for which he assumes pastoral responsibility.

During Vatican II an accredited journalist from the Lithuanian Socialist Soviet Republic gave a humorous orchestral interpretation of Catholic ecumenism. The story goes like this:

> All churches are to play a part in the great Catholic symphony orchestra. The Orthodox are to play first violin, the Anglicans will be given second violin, the Lutherans counterbase, and the young churches from mission lands the drums; all churches are to have at least a minor part. The Jews will be invited to play the harp. The soloists will be from Rome, the Curia will be the agent, and the conductor will always be the pope.49

The obvious conclusion of any evaluation of Roman Catholic ecumenism is that its purpose is to extend an invitation to join the only true church whose unity already exists in the pope. Papal infallibility, supremacy, and jurisdiction is the source of Catholic ecumenism, and a recognition of that source is one of its main goals. Roman Catholic ecumenism is not only unalterably centered in Rome, but in the pope himself.

7

MEDIEVAL THEORISTS AND
PAPAL UNIVERSAL SUPREMACY

The thirteenth century brought the central medieval period of the papacy to its height but also saw the beginning of its decline. If the dramatic event of Canossa (1077), when Henry IV stood outside in the snowy winter for three days and penitently asked for an audience with Pope Gregory VII, who had excommunicated him, is symbolic of the pope's supremacy over the monarch, then equally dramatic is the event at Anagni (1303) when Pope Boniface VIII was taken captive by the French King Philip IV, who by this act indicated the monarch's independence of the pope. In their fight for supremacy over a so-called unified society in which church and state—the spiritual and the temporal—were one, they both failed because they were attempting an impossibility. During the brief periods when the pope gained supremacy, it was generally by subverting spiritual means for the sake of secular goals.

The late medieval period covers the fourteenth and fifteenth centuries and is a transition period. As previously observed, the Babylonian Captivity of the pope (1305-1378) was followed by the Papal Schism (1378-1409) and the Reforming Councils (1409-1447). The Council of Constance (1414-1417) healed the schism but burned Hus at the stake and ordered the bones of Wiclif exhumed, burned, and the ashes thrown into the river, as in the case of Hus. As the ashes were borne to the ocean, so Wiclif's ideas have influenced the world for centuries.

The Conciliar Movement failed to transform the papacy, yet it marked the end of the medieval papacy as a universal power in

European society. The Renaissance popes were, to a large degree, occupied with the politics of the Italian city states.

The city states of Florence, Venice, Milan, and Naples had grown strong and become centers for commerce and culture, and in this process competed with the Papal States. Between them we find continued political interaction with intrigue, conflict, and aggression. The Renaissance popes, like other rulers of this period, patronized the arts and the humanities. Nepotism became widespread in filling positions in the papal government. What Leo X—pope at the time of Luther, and who never perceived the depth of Luther's attack on the church—said when he became pope, other Renaissance popes could have said, "Now we have the papacy, let us enjoy it."

The waning of the influence of the hierarchy and its structure made possible new advances in religious experience and thinking as well as in science. We think of Copernicus and Galileo in the field of astronomy, and Lorenzo Valla and Nicholas of Cusa in linguistic and historical studies. Comparing the Latin Vulgate with the Greek New Testament, Valla demonstrated its many inadequacies. Both Valla and Nicholas demonstrated that the Donation of Constantine was forgery.

New religious experience in the life of the individual was reflected in lay piety and new devotional literature. Meister Eckhart (1377) and Thomas á Kempis in the fifteenth century are typical examples. Next to the Bible, á Kempis' *Imitation of Christ* has been the world's most influential book for half a millennium. It is also next to the Bible in number of copies, editions, and translations.

By preaching and education, John van Ruysbrock, a disciple of Eckhart, and Gerard Groot, one of Ruysbrock's disciples, led out in a spiritual renewal in the Netherlands. Groot founded the Brethren of the Common Life, a fine example of the *Devotio Moderna* (the new devotion) of the time. The Brethren of the Common Life established or reformed several hundred schools, some of which had between one and two thousand students.

The influence of the Brethren of the Common Life was far-reaching. It paved the way for the Reformation of the sixteenth century as they inspired the lives of men such as Martin Luther, John Calvin, and Martin Bucer.

The *Devotio Moderna* of the Netherlands left a heritage which influenced the Puritans in the sixteenth and seventeenth centuries, and the Pilgrim Fathers. We now turn to three "thinkers" who created philosophical, theological, and political concepts which have remained with us to the present. The religious, social, and political climate in which these concepts were formulated is important for a correct evaluation of medieval and modern Roman Catholicism—personified in the pope—Protestantism, and modern democracy.

MARSILIUS OF PADUA:
Prophet of a New Social Order

In the fourteenth century a new note was sounded in the ongoing struggle between pope and emperor, between church and state. "He who struck it was Marsilius of Padua, a thinker whose influence, though greater after his death than in his lifetime, was that of a portent."[1] His book *Defensor Pacis,* "Defender of Peace," set forth most of the ideas which were to become "the creative forces of the modern era." He has been characterized as "a precursor of the Reformation, a theorist of popular sovereignty and constitutional systems, a herald of the modern sovereign state."[2] He "arrived at the fully matured principle of religious toleration."[3] According to M. Emerton, former professor of Ecclesiastical History at Harvard University, "His book has often been called the most remarkable literary product of the Middle Ages, and I am inclined to accept this verdict." He was "the herald of a new world, the prophet of a new social order."[4]

The known facts of Marsilius' life are few. He was born Marsilio dei Mainardini in Padua, Italy, soon after 1270. He was probably educated at the University of Padua, but left for the University of Paris where he occupied the position as rector in the year 1312. In 1316 the pope promised him a canonry in Padua and two years later reserved for him the first vacant benefice, also in Padua.

Marsilius took an active part in the controversy under Pope John XXII (1316-1334), especially with the Spiritual Franciscans who practiced apostolic poverty. In this struggle he was closely associated with William of Occam and took sides with the strict Franciscans against the pope. He was fortunate to escape imprisonment like the others, by fleeing to the court of the Emperor Louis of Bavaria, in whose service he remained as long as it is possible to trace his career. The emperor, who was at that time in conflict with the pope, welcomed Marsilius with enthusiasm. He probably influenced the emperor to march toward Rome in order to seize the imperial crown and set up an anti-pope. Louis named Marsilius papal vicar of Rome, but the expedition ended in failure. Marsilius died not later than 1343, but his memory is preserved in the one great work by which he is known.

Marsilius completed *Defensor Pacis* on June 24, 1324. Its aim was to explain "the principal causes whereby civil peace or tranquility exists and is preserved, and whereby the opposed strife arises and is checked and destroyed."[5] The one singular cause which Marsilius sets forth as the root of strife and the hindrance of peace is "the belief, desire, and undertaking whereby the Roman bishop and his clerical coterie, in particular, are aiming to seize secular rulership and to possess excessive temporal wealth."[6]

Marsilius' aim was, "therefore, with God's help, to expose only this singular cause of strife." He further states:

> For to reiterate the number and nature of those causes which were set forth by Aristotle would be superfluous; but this cause which Aristotle could not have known, and which no one after him who could know it has undertaken to investigate, we wish to unmask so that it may henceforth be readily excluded from all states or cities, and virtuous rulers and subjects live more securely in tranquility.[7]

In his discussion of the state, Marsilius laid down as his first principle that government is established for the purpose of maintaining tranquility.[8] To that end and according to a standard, "a government has to regulate civil human acts."[9] A standard, or law, implies a lawgiver, and Marsilius next discusses who the human legislator is. In the answer to this question he sets forth the basis of his political theory, namely, that the people are the legislator.

In other words, Marsilius rejects the idea that the sovereignty of the state rests with "a certain few" rather than "with the whole of citizens or the weightier multitude thereof." He asserts that "the people, or the multitude composed of all the groups of the polity or city taken together, is more ample than any part of it taken separately, and consequently its judgment is more secure than that of any such part." He further explains: "For the few would not discern or desire the common benefit equally as well as would the entire multitude of the citizens. Indeed, it would be insecure, as we have already shown, to entrust the making of the law to the discretion of the few."[10]

These principles are entirely different from those of the papacy. D'Entreves makes the following comment:

> Only the whole community can adequately value what is just and consonant to the common good, and express it in the form of law; reciprocally, only what the community has laid down in the form of law can and must be the supreme measure of justice...there is nothing left of the Thomist idea that the "state", however "sovereign", is subject to an eternal and absolute order of values, expressed in the body of divine and natural law. The state is the source of law, and its law has to be obeyed not only because it is the only rule to be endowed with coercive power, but because it is in itself the expression of justice.[11]

The same principle that formed the basis of Marsilius' political structure is equally valid for the church: the people themselves are the source of all power.

According to Marsilius "the truest and the most fitting" meaning of the word "church" is "the whole body of the faithful who believe in and invoke the name of Christ, and all the parts of this whole body in any community, even the household."[12] He defines the two ways in which the word "church" was used at his time—the clergy, or those who "preside over the metropolitan or principal church":

This usage was long since brought about by the church of the city of Rome, whose ministers and overseers are the Roman pope and his cardinals. Through custom they have brought it about that they are called the "church" and that one says the "church" has done or received something when it is these men who have done or received or otherwise ordained something.13

Contrary to this concept Marsilius asserts that it is "the believers of Christ, who are the 'Church.'"14 George H. Sabine comments that even the laity, Marsilius says, are churchmen (*viri ecclesiastici*), an expression suggestive of Martin Luther's phrase, "the priesthood of the Christian man."15 In his first discourse Marsilius argues that the source of authority in the state rests with the people. In his second discourse he applies the same principle to the church. Gewirth elaborates on the concept of the church as it had become identified with the pope:

Marsilius' doctrine of the church subverts this entire hierarchic structure. He weakens the continuum between priesthood and God, reverses the superiority of clergy over laymen, and equalizes priests, bishops, and pope in that respect in which their authority had been considered essentially unequal. This revolution is accomplished by the different interpretation which he places upon the definition of the church as the *universatis fidelium*.16

The following pages will illustrate how, according to Marsilius, the fellowship of the believers (*universatis fidelium*) is the true defender of peace because the source of authority is the people.

The advocates of papal supremacy "had argued that either a man must accept the political authority of the Pope or prove himself a heretic by denying the prerogatives of Peter."17 Marsilius returned upon the advocates of the papacy this "their own favourite dilemma" by attacking those prerogatives. Referring to the secular rulership of the pope, he wrote:

Christ gave to the apostles the power to administer
the sacrament of the eucharist... For he did not say:
Do thou [Peter] this and give to the other apostles the
power to do this....

The same view must also be held concerning the
power of the keys.... Christ said to the apostles:
"As my father hath sent me, even so send I
you...receive the Holy Ghost. Whosesoever sins ye
remit, they are remitted unto them... "Nor did Christ
say to Peter: Receive thou the Holy Ghost and then
give it to the others...

Paul was sent with an eminence equal to that of Peter, and not by Peter or by any other apostle, but
immediately by Christ.... [Peter] assumed for himself no authority to settle questions relating to the
preaching of the gospel, with respect to doctrine; but
these questions were settled through the common
deliberation of the apostles and of other more learned
believers [Acts 15]....

The Apostle wrote: "But when Peter was come to
Antioch, I withstood him to the face, because he was
to be blamed, etc." [Gal. 2:11]. Whereon the gloss
according to Jerome: "They communicated nothing
to me, but I communicated unto Peter." And then it
is added: "I opposed him, as an equal. For he
would not have dared do this unless he had known
that he was not unequal."

Peter had no coercive jurisdiction over the other
apostles, any more than conversely, and consequently the successors of the apostles have no coercive jurisdiction over one another.... [Christ] said
unto them: "The kings or princes of the Gentiles
lord it over them, and they that are the greater exercise power upon them. But you not so." Christ
could not have made this denial more clearly....

> Furthermore, the Roman bishop neither is nor ought
> to be called the particular successor of St. Peter on
> account of the laying on of hands, because the Ro-
> man bishop happens to be a man on whom St. Peter
> never laid his hands, either indirectly or directly....

> Concerning St. Peter...I say that it cannot be proved
> through the holy Scripture that he was the bishop of
> Rome in particular, or, what is more, that he was
> ever at Rome....

> ...according to the sacred Scriptures we must hold
> beyond any doubt that St. Paul was the bishop of
> Rome.... That Peter was at Rome I do not deny, but
> I hold it to be quite probable that he did not precede
> Paul there, but rather conversely.[18]

The conclusion, which Marsilius draws in a later chapter, is
that "by virtue of the words of Scripture, therefore, no bishop or
church is the head or leader of the rest as such." But "the only absolute head of the church...is Christ himself."[19]

The only function of the priesthood is that of teaching and
preaching the word of God and administering the sacraments: "The
end of the priesthood, therefore, is to teach and educate men in those
things which, according to the evangelical law, it is necessary to believe, do, and omit in order to attain eternal salvation and avoid misery."[20] Speaking about baptism he says: "And so the ministers of
the sacrament, as of all the others, are the priests as successors of
Christ's apostles."[21] That the priest preaches the word and admin-
isters the sacraments, had "its origin from Christ,"[22] but Marsilius
nullifies the sacerdotal power of the priesthood. A sinner is for-
given completely without an intermediate agency:

> ...in the sinner who is truly penitent, that is, who is
> contrite and has the intention of confessing, God
> alone performs certain things before the confession
> and before all action on the part of the priest. These
> things are the expulsion of guilt, the restoration of

grace, and the forgiving of the debt of eternal damnation.23

The priest's role is thus completely passive:

> For it is God alone who cannot be ignorant as to whose sin is to be pardoned and whose retained; and it is God alone who neither is affected by vicious emotions. ...as a result, if a truly penitent person who duly intended to confess, or had even actually confessed, were not forgiven his sin or guilt and his debt of eternal damnation because of the priest's ignorance, malice, or both, then Christ's evangelical promise, which is an object of faith...would frequently come to naught.24

It is not the laying on of hands by a bishop which, *opus operatum*—"by virtue of the act"—is the essential efficient cause of the priesthood or holy orders. Marsilius writes, the "cause is God or Christ, without mediation, although first there occurs a certain human, as it were preparatory, ministry, like the laying on of hands and the uttering of words, which perhaps effect nothing to this end but which thus precede by virtue of a certain pact or divine ordinance."25 The question of excommunication illustrates Marsilius' concept of church and state; at the same time it throws further light on the power, or lack of power, of the priesthood and the pope. Excommunication by a clergyman does not determine a person's eternal life "because 'God does not always follow the judgment of the church,' that is, of the priests, namely when they judge someone unjustly." Since an excommunicated person "would be harmed most gravely for the status of the present life, because he is defamed and deprived of civil association," then the "cut off from the company of the faithful—pertains to the whole body of the faithful in that community in which the defendant is to be judged by such a judgment."26 The priesthood alone has no power to excommunicate rulers or kings, and the state is not subject to the clergy:

> Moreover, if it pertains to any bishop or priest, either alone or together with a group of clergymen, to ex-

communicate any person without the consent of the whole body of the faithful, then from this it follows that priests or groups of them can remove all states and governments from the kings or rulers who have them. For when any ruler is excommunicated, the multitude subject to him will also be excommunicated if it wishes to obey the excommunicated ruler; and thus the power of every ruler will be broken. But the opposite of this condition was desired by the teacher of the Gentiles in Romans, Chapter 13 and I Timothy, Chapter 6.[27]

An ignorant priest may be a great civil danger—"since priests, through their authority as confessors, often have secret conversations with women"—and may become, for the people, a "danger of eternal death and grave civil harm."[28] On this account, it is important that the right priests be elected, by the right agency, which is, for Marsilius, the "human legislator or the whole body of the faithful":[29]

In perfect communities of believers, the election, assignment, and presentation of persons to be promoted to ecclesiastic orders pertain only to the human legislator or the multitude of the believers in that place over which the minister is to care; and that no bishops or priests, individually or collectively, are allowed to appoint men to such orders without the permission of the legislator or of the ruler by its authority.... The necessity that such things be done by the legislator or the whole body of the citizens is so much the more evident, as any error made in appointing a person to a priestly or other ecclesiastic rank or office of headship is more dangerous than an error with respect to the human law or the appointment of a man to rule in accordance with it.[30]

From this, it is clear that the bishop has no power or authority to elect the priests.

The procedure in composing the council is described in the following way:

> Let all the notable provinces or communities of the
> world, in accordance with the determination of their
> human legislators whether one or many, and ac-
> cording to their proportion in quantity and quality of
> persons, elect faithful men, first priests and then
> non-priests, suitable persons of the most blameless
> lives and the greatest experience in divine law.
> These men are to act as judges in the first sense of
> the word, representing the whole body of the faithful
> by virtue of the authority which these whole bodies
> have granted to them, and they are to assemble at a
> place which is most convenient according to the
> decision of the majority of them, where they are to
> settle those matters pertaining to divine law which
> have appeared doubtful, and which it seems useful,
> expedient, and necessary to define.31

It is not the pope who should convene a general council, but "it pertains only to the authority of the faithful human legislator which lacks a superior, or to the person or persons to whom it has granted such power, to call a general council."32 The pope and the clerical college are elected by "the general council or the faithful human legislator, lacking a superior,"33 who also gives him whatever authority he might have, but it also has the right "to correct him, and even to depose him if it seems expedient to do so."34 Thus the general council remains superior to the pope, and it, and not the pope, represents and preserves the unity of faith. Emerton comments:

> The most impressive feature of this conciliar scheme
> is its representative character. It proceeds from the
> base of the social structure upward to its higher lev-
> els, not from above downward. The unit of repre-
> sentation is the local community acting on the initia-
> tive of its own civil authorities. The delegates, cleri-
> cal as well as lay, are to act in virtue of the authority

derived from the community, not in virtue of any essential quality of their own.35

It is significant that Marsilius' basic principle, which later became the foundation principle for the modern democratic states— that the source of all power is the people—was born in reaction against papal supremacy. This principle is according to Marsilius the defender of peace both in the state as well as in the church. Accordingly, one of the authorities on the political ideas of Marsilius writes, "The permanent significance of Marsilius' ideas is to be found not merely in his opposition to the papal and ecclesiastic institutions of medieval Christendom, but in the entire doctrinal structure which he adduces in support of such opposition."36

Many before and after Marsilius spoke against the universal supremacy of the papacy, but it was the ideological structure of *Defender of the Peace* relating to the basic principles on which the papacy rested its authority, which on one hand made advocates of the papacy curse it, and on the other made it considered a most important work by those who saw in the supremacy of the pope the source of a corrupt church and the root of strife in the state. The reactions to *Defender of the Peace* testify to the impact of its ideology. Clement VI (1342-1352) declared "that he had never read a more shocking heretical book than the *Defensor Pacis*."37 When the popes later condemned such men as Wyclif, Hus, Luther, among others, they charged them with having gotten their ideas from Marsilius. As late as in the Canon Law of 1917 the editor, after having referred to the pope's as "supreme and full power of jurisdiction in the whole Church," comments:

> All those who pervert the essential divine organization of the Church as a perfect society of the monarchical type, necessarily deny the power of the Roman Pontiff. The so-called democrats of the later middle ages (Marsilius, Jandunus, Wiclif, and Hus) were deliberately bent on destroying the pure notion of papal power. But the Jansenists, Gallicans, and Josephinists were also far from the true idea of papal power.38

On the other hand, a man such as Matthias Flacius, professor at Jena from 1557 and a strict Lutheran, wrote in his *Catalogus testium* that, among pre-Reformation works, "there is no more sound, scholarly, bold and pious book against the papal power."39 Leaders of the Protestant Reformation would no doubt agree with Flacius, and in our early discussion of Marsilius we made reference to twentieth-century historians who lauded him.

Marsilius' revolutionary idea, that the priesthood is not essential to the existence of the state, prepared the way for the pre-Reformation. "It was reserved for Wyclif and Hus decisively to demand that the Church should be conceived in a more inward, less external, fashion, as the Community of the Predestinated, and so to prepare the way for that German Reformation which at this very point broke thoroughly away from the medieval Idea of Unity."40

THOMAS AQUINAS: Doctor of Roman Catholicism

In order to better understand the difference, and subsequent conflict, between the basic ideological principles of Roman Catholicism and those of its opponents, it will be helpful to consider, however briefly, the thoughts of Thomas Aquinas (c.1225-1274).

During the thirteenth century a number of universities were founded and Scholasticism reached its highest intellectual achievement in the Middle Ages. In this, the Franciscan and Dominican friars and monks had the great share.

Through social work and preaching, as confessors and inquisitors, teachers and missionaries, the friars were the strength of the papacy during the thirteenth century. The Dominicans had a still more lasting influence when Thomas Aquinas made the papal claim of supremacy a part of Catholic theology: "As for the Church itself, Rome is the mistress and mother of all churches. To obey her is to obey Christ. This is according to the decision of the holy councils and the holy Fathers. The unity of the Church presupposes a supreme centre of authority. To the pope, it belongs to determine what is of faith. Yea, subjection to him is necessary to salvation."41

Aquinas also says that "the secular power is joined to the spiritual, as in the pope, who holds the apex of both authorities, the spiritual and the secular."42

Thomas Aquinas defended ecclesiastical preeminence as a corollary to the doctrine that the basic truths are those of faith and that salvation, man's chief concern, is in the hands of the church. The church is a necessary instrument for achieving man's chief end, and its hegemony is thus given a somewhat Aristotelian justification. If a ruler ignored the decrees of the church he should be excommunicated and his subjects absolved from the necessity of obedience. The authority of the priest was temporal as well as spiritual; the pope was to be obeyed implicitly in all matters of civil welfare as well as in those which related to salvation.

The true end of man is, through a virtuous life, to obtain eternal life. But this cannot be attained through human virtue alone; otherwise the will of the king, as the supreme political power, would be sufficient. But inasmuch as this objective transcends earthly life, it must be reached through the ministry of the priesthood. Although the king is supreme in temporal affairs, even he is subject to the priest. Theologian Reinhold Seeberg writes regarding Aquinas' political theory: "The church attains its summit in the pope. With Aristotle, it was held: 'But the best government of a multitude is that it be ruled by one.'"43

Thomas Aquinas aimed to harmonize reason and revelation, to reconcile the doctrine of the church and rational philosophy, which classic learning had revived. Aquinas represented the scholastic philosophy known as "realism," while Occam stood for "nominalism." It will not be possible to enter into a discussion of these two schools of thought.

Medieval nominalism emphasized the value of the individual, the basis of democracy and Christian individualism. Except for the reaction of nominalism to realism, the Reformation of the sixteenth century and modern democratic states might never have been possible. In this connection it is interesting to note that Thomas Aquinas is the foremost "typical exponent of what a recent historian has called the catholic mind."44

In 1567 Pope Pius V declared Thomas Aquinas to be the "Doctor of the Church." As late as 1879 Pope Leo XIII pronounced, in his encyclical of that year, that the theology of Thomas Aquinas is "the standard of Catholic orthodoxy."45 He was also made patron of Catholic universities, and upon the occasion celebrating his canonization in 1923, Pope Pius XI reemphasized his authority as the theologian of the Roman Catholic Church. Philosophically, John Paul II is a Thomist.

It is obvious that Roman Catholic theology cannot be in harmony with the principles undergirding the Reformation of the sixteenth century as well as modern democratic states, otherwise Roman Catholic theology would have to deny the very essence of their philosophy as represented by Thomas Aquinas. Having referred to Aquinas, Let us now to turn to William of Occam.

WILLIAM OF OCCAM:
Precursor of the Protestant Reformation

William of Occam owes his reputation to his theological and political theories and his definition of the Bible as final authority. He became a distant voice of the Reformation.

Documentary evidence about the life of William of Occam is scanty. He was probably born at Occam in Surrey, England. The date of his birth, usually placed between 1290 and 1300, is uncertain. He joined the Franciscans and was educated at Oxford, where he began the study of theology about the year 1310. He lectured at Oxford from 1315 to 1319 and spent the following years, until 1324, in writing and scholastic disputation.

In 1324 Occam was summoned to the papal court at Avignon to answer charges of unorthodoxy, and fifty-one propositions taken from his writings were condemned. In the controversy between Pope John XXII and the Spiritual Franciscans, Occam took sides with the latter. He defended the doctrine of apostolic poverty and for this he was excommunicated in 1328, but he escaped to the protection of Louis of Bavaria before the order was delivered. He joined the emperor at Pisa and accompanied him to Munich.

Thus began Occam's participation in the struggle between emperor and pope, a struggle assisted by Marsilius of Padua. While some of Occam's polemics against John XXII and his successors, Benedict XII and Clement VI, concerned theological matters, the chief point of the whole dispute was, of course, the right relation of the secular to the ecclesiastical power.[46]

Occam most likely never left Munich, where it is thought he died in 1349, probably a victim of the Black Death. Occam gave a great blow to medieval scholastic theology, as represented by Thomas Aquinas. He taught that the philosopher and theologian must begin with the individual. Only the individual is real. His critical theory of knowledge "is closely bound up with his political theory." His nominalism has "sociologically related suppositions in his theory of knowledge and politics."47

With this basic concept Occam arrived at the principle of representation, also basic for Marsilius: "that which touches all must be acted on by all." It is interesting to note that in arriving at this conclusion his basic concepts are theological and scriptural, and sociologically related to his nominalism, according to which one must begin with the individual inasmuch as only the individual is real. Stephen C. Tornay, an authority on the philosophy of Occam, writes that Occam thus "presents a strong evaluation of the human personality as against the corporate political body, reflecting Occam's emphasis on the concrete and individual in his theory of knowledge as against the general and universal."48

According to Occam all men have the right to participate in the making of laws since they affect all men. But they can delegate this right to certain persons, for example princes, and in doing so surrender to them only such rights as they themselves have. The prince may not exceed these rights and may only do such things as are not contrary to divine or natural law, otherwise the right of resistance by those who have surrendered their rights comes into force.49

Occam's ideas on the relationship between church and state are most succinctly set forth in a short "compendium" called *De Imperatorum et Pontificium Potestate* written at the close of his life in 1346 or 1347.50 After a short preface Occam goes to the heart of his subject by the assertion that, in appointing the apostle Peter head of the believers, Christ did not give him plenary power in temporal matters or plenitude of power—as proved by reason and by Scripture (2 Tim. 2:4; Matt. 20:25). Neither did Christ grant Peter plenitude of power in spiritual matters, for then the pope could impose on the faithful heavy burdens "inconsistent with the liberty of the law of the gospel."

Occam strongly emphasizes that the apostolic principle, which should be followed by the pope and the bishops, is that of serving the church spiritually.51 "It belongs to the pope, even as to all bishops in general, as the canons bear witness, to further the reading, speaking, preaching of the word of God and divine worship and all those things that are necessary and proper to Christians for the attainment of eternal life and do not exist among unbelievers." Since the clergy cannot be occupied with secular matters, Occam encourages the idea that laymen care for secular business connected with the administration of the church.52

Characteristic is Occam's constant appeal to Scripture as the final source of authority. No doctrine not rooted in holy Scripture should be acknowledged as catholic and necessary to salvation; neither the church nor the pope could make new articles of faith. In this way he contributed to upsetting the medieval theory of the seat of authority and assailed the traditional doctrines of his time. In the introduction to his last treatise he wrote: "Yet let all men hold this as certain: that in matters of faith and of knowledge, one evident reason or one authority of discipline reasonably understood will move me more than the assertion of the whole world of mortal men...."53

Occam was a distant voice of the Reformation; no wonder Luther called him "my dear master," and said "'I am of the Occamist faction.'" Occam "stands in a direct relation to the greatest event of the succeeding age, the Reformation....he was no forerunner for Luther as a Reformer, but he was one of the factors without which the Reformation would have been impossible."54

Marsilius' and Occam's ideas of representation in the church are of the highest significance. For more than a century they were the core of violent debate, in the attempt to transform the papacy from an absolute into a constitutional monarchy reflected in the Conciliar Movement and the Reforming Councils—to all of which the Vatican Council of 1870 gave a final "no." How the Reformation of the sixteenth century and the post-Reformation era answered the challenge of Marsilius and Occam is the subject of the following pages.

THE PROTESTANT FATHERS
ON CHURCH-STATE RELATIONS

Luther began his reformatory activities by proclaiming the doctrine of *sola fide* (by faith alone), which called for a reformation of the church, not only in doctrine but also in structure. This, in turn, led to a reform in the concept of the state, anticipated by the theories of Marsilius and Occam, which became part and parcel of the revolt against the papacy. It has been pointed out that "It was Luther who accomplished the true deliverance of the State; he achieved it by removing the differentiation between ecclesiastically good works and worldly activities and by limiting religion and the Church to their proper sphere." Further, "Considered by itself the Reformation also signifies the negation of the universal empire of the Middle Ages," and "The decision which lay in the final elimination of all claims of sovereignty of the Church over the State was the victory of the modern State whose sovereignty could already be proclaimed at the end of the sixteenth century. Luther brought about this decision."[55]

On the subject of church-state relations Luther wrote a book early in the year 1523. On the basis of Christ's words "Render therefore unto Caesar the things which are Caesar's; and unto God the things that are God's" (Acts 22:21). Luther made a sharp distinction between church and state:

God has ordained two governments among the children of Adam,—the reign of God under Christ, and the reign of the world under the civil magistrate, each with its own laws and rights. The laws of the reign of the world extend no further than body and goods and the external affairs on earth. But over the soul God can and will allow no one to rule but himself alone. Therefore where the worldly government dares to give laws to the soul, it invades the reign of God, and only seduces and corrupts the soul. This we shall make so clear that our noblemen, princes, and bishops may see what fools they are if they will

force people with their laws and commandments to
believe this or that.[56]

The church historian Philip Schaff called this statement by
Luther "a prophetic anticipation of the American separation of
church and state."[57]

According to Luther the power of the church is limited to the
ministry of the Word. For a time Luther conceived of the church as
congregational in form, as a voluntary group of committed Christians, but he later changed his concept of the church, church-state
relations, and religious liberty—a change tragic for the spiritual development of the Reformation. Luther's faith in the "common man"
was somewhat shaken by the Peasant War. For political reasons he
placed the church under the general supervision of the state, which
then to a large degree dominated the church. The price Luther paid
for the help of the territorial princes was high. Karl Holl, a defender
of Luther, admits this and adds that the "best energies of the Reformation were kept down through this development or they were
forced to develop alongside and apart from the Church."[58]

An outstanding American Lutheran scholar, the late Professor J. L. Neve, has said that the establishment of Lutheran territorial
churches "laid the foundation for a continuing injury to Lutheranism
from which Germany is suffering to this present day."[59]

As the years went by Lutherans organized territorial
churches and brought public worship into harmony with Protestant
beliefs, but by 1529 Emperor Charles V had obtained peace in the
empire and turned his attention to the Lutheran revolt. The Diet of
Speyer, in 1529, stated that Lutherans would not be tolerated in
Catholic districts, but Catholics would have full rights of worship,
property, and income in Lutheran districts. The Lutherans made a
formal protest, which led to their designation as "Protestants." Thus
the very name "Protestantism" was coined in a struggle against inequality in the arrangement which demanded liberty for Catholics
but denied it to the Lutherans. The opposition of the Lutherans at
the Diet of Speyer was not only a protest against inequality but also
a testimony to the basic truths of the gospel and their bearing upon
social equality independent of religious affiliation. The word
Protestantism combined the twin ideas of "protest" and "testify."

A second generation reformer, John Calvin, built on Luther's foundation. In his *Institutes of the Christian Religion* Calvin emphasizes that, according to the Word of God, "By me kings reign and princes decree justice" (Prov. 8:15), and "There is no power but of God: the powers that be are ordained of God" (Rom. 13:1).60 He states the duty of non-resistance as follows:

> Wherefore, if we are cruelly tormented by a savage, if we are rapaciously pillaged by an avaricious or luxurious, if we are neglected by a sluggish, if in short, we are persecuted for righteousness' sake by an impious and sacrilegious prince, let us first call up the remembrance of our faults, which doubtless the Lord is chastising by such scourges. In this way humility will curb our impatience. And let us reflect that it belongs not to us to cure these evils, that all that remains for us is to implore the help of the Lord, in whose hands are the hearts of kings, and inclinations of kingdoms.61

On the other hand Calvin emphatically states that a person "ought to obey God rather than men," and not obey magistrates if it means disobeying God. He sought to transform the civil government of Geneva into harmony with the Law of God, thus making the magistrates real servants of the Lord. When and where that was not accomplished, he left the way open for political resistance. The Huguenots in France, Knox in Scotland, and the Puritans in England all adopted this concept.

Calvin was greatly opposed to any interference by the civil powers in the internal affairs of the church, but his idea that Christ should govern the magistrates tied the state to the church in what may be styled a theocracy or bibliocracy. This form of government also led to intolerance in Geneva itself and later among the Puritans in the States of New England. Philip Schaff writes:

> The union of church and state accounts for the persecution of papists, heretics, and Jews; and all the Reformers justified persecution to the extent of de-

position and exile, some even to the extent of death, as in the case of Servetus.

The modern progress of the principle of toleration and religious liberty goes hand in hand with the loosening of the bond of union between church and state.62

In spite of all the intolerance in Geneva, Jean Jacques Rousseau wrote in his *Social Contract* two centuries after Calvin's day:

Those who consider Calvin only as a theologian fail to recognize the breadth of his genius. The editing of our wise laws, in which he had a large share, does him as much honor as his *Institutes*. Whatever revolution time may bring in our religion, so long as the love of country and liberty is not extinct among us, the memory of this great man will be held in reverence.63

In his theocratic concept Calvin was closer to Rome than Luther, but in his presbyterian form of church organization, he gave a significance to the individual "which of necessity leads to a democratic conception and development of the entire ecclesiastical system."64 In the various councils in Geneva, laymen, teachers, and ministers decided together on disciplinary matters. Calvin also gave to the local congregation a voice in the choice of its officers. Nevertheless, it was only with the presbyterian and congregational forms of church government, in a society with absolute separation of church and state, that religious liberty and modern democracy could develop.

8

THE DEVELOPMENT OF RELIGIOUS LIBERTY

Man's constitutive relationship with God is one of freedom, for man is a self-conscious moral being. The gospel of Jesus Christ tells us what true humanness and genuine freedom mean, and it points out the source of their actualization. Jesus Christ said: "You will know the truth, and the truth will make you free. If, therefore the Son will make you free, you will be free indeed" (John 8:32,36).

At the beginning of the second World War, William Temple very succinctly expressed the relationship between human rights and the dignity and worth of man as it is reflected in the act of redemption by Jesus Christ. Wrote Archbishop Temple: "There can be no Rights of Man except on the basis of faith in God. But if God is real, and all men are his sons, that is the true worth of everyone of them. My worth is what I am worth to God; and that is a marvellous great deal, for Christ died for me. Thus, incidentally, what gives to each of us his highest worth gives the same worth to everyone; in all that matters most, we are all equal."[1]

There is a relationship between Christian freedom and freedom at large. G. C. Berkouwer quotes H. Schlier as saying: "In the Christian idea of freedom the breakthrough to real freedom occurs. If we comprehend what freedom is in its Christian meaning, then we have also grasped the source of every freedom."[2]

Christian freedom is freedom for obedience to God, and we must assert that freedom by saying: "We must obey God rather than man" (Acts 5:29). Absence of coercion is sometimes referred to as negative freedom, but it is merely toleration, not freedom.

In the history of freedom we find that the claim for religious liberty has often opened the door for political and social freedom. Saying this we must first confess that through the centuries Christians forced the conscience of others, manifested intolerance, and persecuted in order to enforce religious uniformity in alliance with the political powers. Next, it must be acknowledged that this is true of Catholics and Protestants alike.

THE PROTESTANT REFORMERS AND RELIGIOUS LIBERTY

At the Diet of Worms in 1521 Luther championed religious liberty when he said, "To act against our conscience is neither safe of us nor open to us. On this I take my stand. I can do no other. God help me. Amen." During the early years of the Reformation he made many statements affirming religious liberty, such as:

> Princes are not to be obeyed when they command submission to superstitious errors but their aid is not to be invoked in support of the Word of God....
>
> Belief is a free thing which cannot be enforced....
>
> Heresy is a spiritual thing which no iron can hew down, no fire burn, no water drown....
>
> See, then, what mad folk we have so long been, who have wished to force the Turk to the faith with the sword, the heretic with fire, and the Jews with death, to root out the tares with our own power, as if we were the people who could rule over hearts and spirits and make them religious and good, which God's Word alone must do.3

In later years when facing his opponents Luther displayed a spirit of intolerance and harshness toward those who differed from him. This is evident with respect to Baptists, Roman Catholics, and Jews alike. His intimate associate, the otherwise mild Melanchthon, wrote about the Baptists in 1530: "I am now of the opinion that

persons who defend an article of doctrine which, though not insur-
rectory, is openly blasphemous should be put to death by the authorities, for these must punish open blasphemy as much as other
public crimes. The law of Moses teaches us this."4

At the request of Philip of Hesse the Wittenberg theologians
wrote a statement about the Baptists, dated June 5, 1536.
According to this document the magistrate is responsible "to restrain
and punish false teaching in public, improper Divine service, and
heresies, in his own district, and in the case of persons over whom
he has rule." The document specifically states:

> Where now the Anabaptists have articles contrary to
> the secular government, it is so much the easier to
> judge; for there is no doubt that in such cases the ob-
> stinate should be punished as rebellious. But where
> someone has *articles on spiritual matters alone*, such
> as *infant baptism*, original sin, and unnecessary
> division, because these articles also are important
> ...*we conclude that in these cases also the obstinate
> may be put to death.*

To this statement Luther added with his own hand:

> Seeing that our gracious Landgrave reports that cer-
> tain leaders and teachers of the Anabaptists are in
> prison, who are to be banished (that is, who had
> been banished from the land) and had not kept their
> promise, Your Princely Grace may, on the ground
> that they have become disobedient and have not kept
> their promise or oath, with a good conscience, have
> them *punished with the sword.*5

Luther was very severe in his judgment of Zwingli, with
whom he disagreed about the Lord's Supper. Upon learning of the
defeat and death of Zwingli by the Catholics he wrote: "I confess
for myself that I hold Zwingli, with all his teaching, as unchristian,
and he holds and teaches no item of the Christian faith aright, and is
become seven times worse than if he were a Papist."6 The Lutheran
state church became a persecuting church.

The type of church-state relationship that developed in Lutheran territories is called Erastianism, after a Swiss theologian of the sixteenth century who maintained that the church should be subject to the state. The Reformation in England established the same principle. England secured political and religious freedom from the papacy, but the ruling monarch became the supreme ruler or governor of the church, and in many ways made the church subservient to the state. Those who did not conform to the new establishment were persecuted. It is a paradox that before the Reformation the pope was the supreme ruler in the church, and the church was over the state, but after the Reformation the state was over the church and the monarch the supreme governor of the church. This relationship between church and state has been called Caesaropapacy after the Eastern emperors who ruled over the church as popes.

The Swiss reformers were, generally speaking, intolerant. Zwingli approved the drowning of the Anabaptists. According to one Protestant scholar, "If Calvin ever wrote anything in favor of religious liberty, it was a typographic error."[7]

The classic example of Calvin's persecution is that of Michael Servetus, who held anti-trinitarian views. On October 27, 1553, having refused to renounce his teachings, he was burned at the stake along with his books. His last words were: "O Jesus, thou son of the eternal God, have pity on me." Calvin defended the execution of Servetus in a work published in both Latin and French early in 1554, in which he said of the execution of Servetus: "It was the law of the Holy Roman Empire, the Code of Justinian, that prescribed the penalty of death for a denial of the Trinity and a repetition of baptism."[8] The Reformation thus resorted to laws which, since the time of Justinian, had provided for secular enforcement of religious doctrine and secular punishment of those at variance with its state-supported religion.

As for the history of religious liberty, it is, however, true to say that the Reformation erected a platform on which it was possible to develop a more perfect liberty. During the early period of the Reformation the reformers advocated liberty of conscience as well as obedience to God as man's primary duty. The doctrines of the Bible as sole authority in matters of faith, justification by faith, the priesthood of all believers, and the participation of the laity in church government, together with the Protestant concept of Christ as sole head of the church, created a platform on which the champions of religious liberty could further their cause.

On the other hand, the reformers' alliance with the state led to intolerance. According to Philip Schaff: "Protestant persecution differs from papal persecution in extent and degree, but not in principle....Protestant persecution is even less excusable than Roman Catholic persecution, because it is inconsistent and contrary to the first principle of the Reformation, which must stand or fall with liberty."9

Referring to the great Reformation monument in Geneva, Roland H. Bainton writes: "The paradox of the monument is that it includes men who would have destroyed each other had they met in life." John Calvin, Theodore Beza, William Farel, and John Knox stand together as a part of the movement representing the Reformation in Geneva. All four were persecutors. "John Calvin was responsible for the execution of Michael Servetus at the stake. Farel attended the execution. Beza justified the holocaust, and John Knox applauded."10 Both the Lutheran and the English state churches persecuted dissenters. The Protestant Reformation of the sixteenth century did not solve the problem of religious liberty. Intolerance and brutal force as represented by the sword continued in the church.

The full development of religious liberty is not to be found among the major churches of the Reformation, but the Free Church movement of the sixteenth and seventeenth centuries.

RELIGIOUS LIBERTY AND GERMANY

The Protestant Reformation of the sixteenth century separated the Lutheran and Anglican churches from Rome, but only to make the church subject to the state. At the Peace of Augsburg in 1555 equal rights in the empire were extended to Catholics and Lutherans, but no other evangelicals were recognized. Only one faith would be permitted in a given territory—that of the ruling prince. This principle is usually defined as *cuius regio, eius religio* (each region, or territory, his religion), that is, the religion of the ruling prince or monarch was to be that of its inhabitants. On the continent this principal was to a large degree the cause of the political-religious upheaval known as the Thirty Years War (1618-1648). In 1648 the Peace of Westphalia confirmed the right of both Catholics and Lutherans to exist, and the Reformed Church, which had won many followers in Germany, was accorded the same right for the first time. No other Christian group, however, was granted the right to exist.

As the evil of the alliance between the church and the state became apparent, Protestant groups outside the Lutheran and the Reformed Churches felt more and more strongly that outward separation from the state church did not guarantee inward liberation from the influence and principles of the theology and unbiblical ecclesiasticism of the Middle Ages. Thus they concluded that the reformers' alliance with the state was only half-way reform, and as a result they advocated the principle of a free church and religious liberty. Their struggle for religious liberty was closely bound up with the basic principles of the gospel. These Protestant groups went through many decades of trial before toleration was granted them, and centuries had to pass before religious liberty and its corollary, the separation of church and state, became a reality in the New World.

In Germany the first official edict of toleration and religious liberty was issued in 1849, and incorporated in the German constitution of 1871. Some of the German monarchs prior to that had exercised toleration. Frederick the Great (1712-1786), whose well-known motto was, "In my dominions everybody is at liberty to get saved after his own fashion," extended a large measure of liberty. He said: "All that a ruler can require of his subjects is that they be good citizens. False zeal for religion is a tyrant that depopulates the provinces; toleration is a loving mother that nurses them and promotes their welfare." Philip Schaff comments:

> Frederick deemed it the greatest perverseness in a
> ruler to demand that all should think alike or to en-
> force this by punishment. There never will be a so-
> ciety of uniformity of opinions. The prince has no
> authority over the opinions of citizens. His business
> is to guard the welfare of society, not to oppress the

freedom of its members. The welfare of society requires toleration, which is the basis of national prosperity. With liberty of worship everybody is pleased, but persecution has caused the bloodiest, the longest, and the most destructive wars. Religious toleration, therefore, is demanded both by natural right and State policy.11

In 1871 the Protestant King of Prussia issued the first decree of religious liberty, marking "the greatest epoch in the political history of Germany since the establishment of the Holy Roman Empire by Charlemagne in league with Pope Leo III., A.D. 800. This new Empire had no official connection with any Church, and leaves the subject of religion to the several States of which it was composed."12 Yet, the Lutheran church remained in alliance with the state by the fact that it received its financial support from the treasury of the state. It ought always to be remembered that self-support and self-government are inseparable. This principle was first realized in the United States of America.

RELIGIOUS LIBERTY AND FRANCE

Some of the darkest pages in the history of toleration and religious liberty were written in France. The Huguenots, as Protestants were called in France, suffered more than any of the other major Protestant groups. The horrible massacre of St. Bartholomew's Day in 1572, the details of which are well known, is only one instance of what was going on almost constantly on a smaller scale for nearly half a century. The French Protestants held their first national synod in 1559 and adopted the *French Confession of Faith*. Their system of church order was based upon that of Calvin, but more congregational and democratic in character.

In spite of the massacre of St. Bartholomew, more and more Frenchmen embraced the Protestant faith. At the close of the sixteenth century the Huguenots numbered more than one million, or one-twentieth of the population. The political leader of the Huguenots was Henry of Navarre, who gave up his Protestant faith and professed the Catholic faith in 1595 in order to become king.

His words "Paris is worth a mass" have become a saying, and for his former Protestant friends, a small but influential minority, he issued the Edict of Nantes in 1598. The main provision of this edict has been summarized thus:

> The Huguenots were guaranteed full personal liberty in any part of France, without molestation on account of their religious opinions, and made eligible to all secular offices of trust, honor, or emolument.... They have free access to the schools, colleges, and hospitals; they may establish their own schools and universities, and publish religious books in the places where their worship is allowed; portions of the public cemetaries...are assigned to them for the peaceful burial of their dead; they are authorized to hold consistories, colloquies, provincial and national synods.13

The Edict of Nantes did not grant religious liberty; it recognized the liberty of private conscience, but although it restricted the liberty of public worship it nevertheless stands among the great monuments of the European quest for freedom.14 Effectiveness of the provisions of the Edict of Nantes depended almost entirely on the will of the ruling monarch. One by one the privileges of the Protestants were abridged, and their condition became gradually more and more intolerable until the revocation of the Edict of Nantes by Louis XIV in 1685. This edict ordered all Protestant churches and private schools destroyed. The Huguenots were forbidden to gather for religious services; their children were to be baptized by a Catholic priest and brought up as Catholics.15

The Edict of Revocation was followed through to the bitter end with utmost vigor. The prisons were filled with the Huguenots, and a large number were tortured to death. These evils have been called "the darkest days in the history of France and the history of liberty." The number of Huguenots who left France has been estimated at from 300,000 to 400,000. They were the ablest, wealthiest and most enterprising Frenchmen. According to Philip Schaff:

The Revocation was a moral crime, a political blunder, and a national disaster. It deprived France of many thousands of her best citizens, ruined her manufacturers and commerce, subjected her for a long time to the pillage of the dragoons, brought untold misery upon individuals, families, and communities, armed parents against children and children against parents, covered the land with hypocrisy, perjury, and sacrilege, roused the indignation of the Protestant world, filled the refugees with hatred of their native country, and was the remote cause of the French Revolution.16

The pope and the Roman Catholic hierarchy praised Louis XIV for the revocation of the Edict of Nantes, but persecution, Catholic tyranny, and the work of the Jesuits provoked infidelity and led to the destruction of the church during the French Revolution. The political leaders of the Revolution knew Christianity only in the form of political despotism it had taken in France, and therefore hated the Roman Church.

"Crush the wretch," meaning the Catholic Church, was the battle cry of the Revolution. The growth of the spirit of liberty during the second half of the eighteenth century manifested itself in the writings of such men as Voltaire, Rousseau, and Turgot. Voltaire advocated "toleration as a right of justice, a duty of humanity, a condition of the prosperity of the State, and as the only basis of peace between the State and religion, and the different religions. Toleration promotes population. It alone makes society endurable. The Christian religion, he thought, ought to be the most tolerant, because Christians have been the most intolerant among men."17

In its Constitution of the year 1793 the Revolutionary Government stated in Article VII: "The right to express one's thoughts and opinions by means of the press or in any other manner, the right to assemble peaceably, the free pursuit of religion, can not be forbidden."18 The thought of this Article is similar to that of the First Amendment of the American Constitution.

It is significant that 1260 years after Emperor Justinian had made the bishop of Rome the head of all Christendom, and thus the custodian of Roman and canon law in the West, France abolished the canon law, took the pope into captivity, and established the free exercise of religion. It is tragic that a group of deists established the principle of religious liberty, but the verdict of history made the decision inevitable.

When Napoleon came to power he concluded a concordat with the pope that involved the restoration of the Roman Catholic Church in France. It ordered the resignation of all French bishops, declared Napoleon's right as first consul to nominate bishops, provided for payment of the clergy out of the State treasury, and required them to obey the civil government. Napoleon placed the Protestants on a parity with Roman Catholics. On the part of the government this involved protection, financial support, and control in matters of discipline and doctrine. Thus toleration but not religious liberty was the final outcome in France.

RELIGIOUS LIBERTY AND ENGLAND

England's Act of Toleration of 1689 saved her from a revolution like the one in France. The Protestant and Evangelical churches gave her the moral strength, which to a large degree accounts for her national strength and success during the eighteenth and nineteenth centuries.

During the Reformation period the ruling monarch was the supreme authority in the English Church. Henry VIII (1509-1547) persecuted Protestant dissenters and Roman Catholics alike, depending on his changing moods. During the reign of his Protestant son Edward VI (1547-1553) persecution practically ceased, but under Queen Mary (1553 -1558) the Protestants suffered severe martyrdom. The Religious Settlement of Queen Elizabeth (1558-1603) did not include either Puritans or Roman Catholics. James I (1603-1625) and Charles I (1625-1649) followed the line laid down by Queen Elizabeth, but the Puritan forces of opposition that had developed during her reign grew ever stronger as the civil and ecclesiastical administration became more and more despotic.

After the execution of Charles I in 1649, Cromwell gave to the major Evangelical groups equality to the extent that they were not suspected of disloyalty. Congregationalist, Presbyterian, and

Evangelical churchmen were eligible to become ministers in the parish churches, but Catholics and Unitarians were excluded. The Westminster Confession of 1644—a Presbyterian creed for the whole of Britain—stated that heretics "may lawfully be called to account, and proceeded against by the censures of the Church and by the power of the Civil Magistrate."[19] The Presbyterians thus sought to establish a theocracy, with a disregard of the right of conscience equal to that of the monarchy and the episcopacy. Only the Quakers and the Baptists consistently advocated universal toleration in their creeds.

Following the temporary triumph of the Independents under Cromwell and the Commonwealth (1649-1660) came the reactionary reigns of Charles II and James II. Charles II (1660-1685) renewed the Elizabethan Act of Uniformity and passed several other intolerant acts against dissenters. The Act of Uniformity required every minister to subscribe to the Book of Common Prayer, and as a result more than 2,000 Presbyterian, Congregational, and Baptist ministers were driven from their churches. Any person who attended a religious service of more than five persons not conducted after the ritual of the Church of England was punished. Noble men such as John Bunyan were treated as criminals, thrown into prison, and many fled the country.

With a view to promoting the interests of Roman Catholics, King James II (1685-1688) relaxed the oppressive acts of his predecessor, but the dissenters were unwilling to benefit from this concession, fearing that it might result in the restoration of Roman Catholicism. Finally the nation revolted against the despotism of its last two kings, and the Glorious (and bloodless) Revolution of 1688 brought William of Orange to the English throne. He was disposed to tolerate differences of religious opinion, and in 1689, four years after Louis XIV had revoked the Edict of Nantes, he issued his Edict of Toleration. The significance of this Act has been summarized as follows:

> The Act of Toleration left the Church of England unchanged, and in possession of all her endowments, rights, and privileges, but it limited her jurisdiction, so that she ceased from that time on to be coextensive

with the nation. It gave the orthodox Protestant Dissenters, under certain conditions and restrictions, a legal existence, and the right of public worship and self-government, dependent upon self-support (for these two are inseparably connected). Its benefit extended to Presbyterians, Independents, Baptists, and Quakers, but to no others. It stopped the persecution against them, but not against Unitarians and Roman Catholics, who are expressly excluded from the benefit of the Act by Section XVII.20

The Act of Toleration was limited, however, and has often been called an act of intolerance against Unitarians and Roman Catholics. The Unitarians eventually secured toleration in 1813 and the Roman Catholics in 1829, but Jews not until 1858.

RELIGIOUS LIBERTY AND VATICAN COUNCIL II

On the second to the last day of Vatican Council II (Dec. 7, 1965) the Declaration on Religious Freedom (*Dignitatis Humanae*) was promulgated. By supporting religious freedom for all it brought the Roman Catholic Church into harmony with the general development and appreciation for religious liberty as the concept had developed during the past centuries and been expressed in the Universal Declaration of Human Rights by the United Nations in 1948.

Outlining the general principles of religious freedom, the Declaration on Religious Freedom begins by expressing the following assertions:

This Vatican Synod declares that the human person has a right to religious freedom. This freedom means that all men are to be immune from coercion on the part of individuals or of social groups and of any human power, in such wise that in matters religious no one is to be forced to act in a manner contrary to his own beliefs. Nor is anyone to be restrained from acting in accordance with his own beliefs, whether privately or publicly, whether alone or in association with others, within due limits.

The Synod further declares that the right to religious freedom has its foundations in the very dignity of the human person, as this dignity is known through the revealed Word of God and by reason itself. This right of the human person to religious freedom is to be recognized in the constitutional law whereby society is governed. Thus it is to become a civil right.21

This introduction, and the document as a whole, is unique in the sense that it is the first official Roman Catholic statement of its kind. In spirit and letter it represents a great step forward. The principles expressed are different from those previously promulgated. The document is specifically addressed to the whole world. Pope John XXIII had opened the way for a change, and at a critical point in the discussions Pope Paul VI gave his support to the great number of Council fathers who favored it. The American bishops played an active leadership role. The present pope, John Paul II, has confirmed the concept of religious freedom on several occasions.

In an address at the Lateran University, which had sponsored a colloquium on the theme "Basic Rights of the Human Person and Religious Freedom," the pope said:

What foundation can we offer as a basis upon which man's rights can flourish? Without doubt, that basis is the dignity of the human person.... It is in this dignity of the human person that human rights find their immediate source. And it is respect for this dignity which gives rise to their effective protection.... Now among man's rights there is justly listed the right to religious freedom; rather it is the most fundamental, since the dignity of every person has its first source in his or her essential relationship with God the Creator and Father, in whose likeness and image the human person was created, since he or she is endowed with intelligence and freedom.... Certainly the limitation of the religious freedom of individuals and communities not only is a painful experience, but above all it wounds man's very dignity, regardless of the religion professed or of the vision one has of the world.22

The positive aspects of the document have been aptly summarized by Raymond F. Cottrell, one of the official journalists attending the council. He writes:

As it now stands, the declaration on religious liberty bases man's right to religious freedom on the growing consciousness of human dignity and the recognition that he should be free from all forms of coercion in order to discharge his duty toward God. No one should be forced to act, or be prevented from acting, according to his conscience. This right belongs to religious groups as well as to individuals. Civil authority is out of bounds if it interferes in any way with man's relationship to God, unless he disturbs the public peace, violates public morality, or infringes on the equal rights of others. It is said to be the desire of the council that all governments recognize the equal rights of all men to religious liberty, and surround this right with effective safeguards. Neither individuals nor groups are to be hampered in publicly teaching and witnessing to their religious faith.23

Whatever loopholes the document contains, and there are some, it must be appreciated by all who stand for religious liberty. In a congenial atmosphere, dialogue has been made possible, and in the struggle for advancement of religious freedom a Catholic document can now be quoted endorsing this vital principle.

As a document, the Declaration on Religious Freedom had a somewhat checkered history during the council. It went through six revisions. Originally, the topic was not listed among the subjects to be dealt with. The subject came up and was dealt with as part of the decree on ecumenism. As such, it was debated for eleven days during the second session and became a schema by itself. The suggestion from the "conservatives" that the schema needed further study before being voted on, led to the signing of a petition asking the pope to intervene, and this he did. When the vote was taken, one thousand nine hundred and ninety-seven voted for and two hundred twenty-four against. In view of the fact that the pope had encouraged the acceptance of the document, the opposition was stronger than the figures indicate.

Further, there are statements in the document which could be considered as loopholes and used by those who opposed it. On the other hand, those who were in favor of the document also realized that the document was not final but the first step toward a further development. No doubt both the progressives and the conservatives hope the development will go their way.

Father John Courtney Murray, S.J., of America was a key person in formulating and promoting the religious freedom schema. He admits in a preface to the document that "the Declaration deals only with the minor issue of religious freedom in the technical secular sense," and the "conciliar affirmation of the principle of freedom was narrowly limited—in the text." He also confirms that the schema was

> the most controversial document of the whole Council, largely because it raised with sharp emphasis the issue that lay continually below the surface of all the conciliar debates—the issue of the development of doctrine. The notion of development, not the notion of religious freedom, was the real sticking-point for many of those who opposed the Declaration even to the end. The course of the development between the *Syllabus of Errors* (1864) and *Dignitatis Humanae Personae* (1965) still remains to be explained by theologians. But the Council formally sanctioned the validity of the development itself; and this was a doctrinal event of high importance for theological thought in many other areas.[24]

Franklin H. Littel, a Protestant professor of church history, made a written response to the schema in which he says: "In one major dimension, the logic of religious freedom remains undeveloped. The theme is thoroughly elaborated in reference to the natural rights of persons and associations. It is soundly grounded in the system of belief of the Church. The implications for the nature of a just government are less thoroughly treated."[25]

A few days after the vote was taken in favor of the religious freedom document, the *Christian Science Monitor* made an objective evaluation of it. It stated that while the document "makes a tremendous step forward for the Catholic Church on this issue, the Declaration with its reservations is still a far cry from the advanced religious liberty found in the United States. It allows, for example, for a continuation of a state church." It was further noted that "the concordat whereby a sovereign state grants the Catholic Church special privileges is considered entirely proper. The provision that no one should be forced to act or be prevented from acting according to his conscience, except where his action would infringe public morality, public order, or the rights of others, leaves the door open for possible continued religious harassment and persecution."[26] The Vatican document clearly asserts: "We believe that this one true religion subsists in the catholic and apostolic Church, to which the Lord Jesus committed the duty of spreading it abroad among all men." Further, religious liberty "leaves untouched traditional Catholic doctrine on the moral duty of men and societies toward the true religion and toward the one Church of Christ."[27] The implication of the last statement can have far-reaching consequences. While other churches may consider themselves as the true church, they would not claim a special recognition.

Dr. A. T. Carillo de Albornoz, a former Roman Catholic who joined the Anglican Church, was for several years on the staff of the World Council of Churches in Geneva and served its section for religious liberty. The statement on religious liberty issued by the World Council of Churches owes much to him. Regarding the problem of inequality in Vatican documents he writes: "Precisely because objective truth has no place in matters of civil religious liberty, we do not think that this statement can have practical results other than the uneasiness of having (in a highly ecumenical document) a highly anti-ecumenical statement."28

No doubt with reference to countries where Roman Catholicism is the state religion or has a special preferential position the schema on religious liberty reads: "If, in view of peculiar circumstances obtaining among certain peoples, special legal recognition is given in the constitutional order of society to one religious body, it is at the same time imperative that the right of all citizens and religious bodies to religious freedom should be recognized and made effective in practice."29 The positive aspect is, of course, that the minority groups have religious freedom, but it is on a different level than that of the Catholic Church. This means inequality and is not genuine religious liberty; yet, Father Murray writes: "This paragraph is carefully phrased. The Council did not wish to condemn the institution of 'establishment,' the notion of a 'religion of the state.' A respectable opinion maintains that the institution is compatible with full religious freedom. On the other hand, the Council did not wish to canonize the institution."30

Here is detected a reasoning which has become more and more pronounced in the United States of America, namely, religious liberty could function without absolute separation of church and state, even with preferential treatment. Reference could be made to the diplomatic relations between the United States of America and the Holy See and tax subsidies to church schools. The schema correctly states that parents "have the right to determine, in accordance with their own religious beliefs, the kind of religious education that their children are to receive." As a consequence—and we will agree—the government "must acknowledge the right of parents to make genuinely free choice of schools and of other means of education." Next references are made to educational subsidies by the state when it states: "The use of this freedom of choice is not to be made a reason for imposing unjust burdens on parents," and it adds, "whether directly or indirectly."31

The government's duty to support religion is brought in, may we say, through a back door. The government is responsible for the welfare of society as such. "Therefore, the care of the right to religious freedom devolves upon the people as a whole, upon social groups, upon government, and upon the Church and other religious Communities, in virtue of the duty of all toward the common welfare, and in the manner proper to each."[32] The following comment is made to this part of the schema by Father Murray, who writes: "The concern of the Council was, first, to make entirely clear the duty of government toward religious freedom as a human right, and secondly, to make sufficiently clear the function of government with regard to religion itself as a perfection of the human person and as a social value."[33]

Inherent in the American concept of a free church in a free state—or the separation of church and state—is the inescapability of self-support and self-government. It should always be remembered that religious liberty means more than freedom from intolerance and persecution; it grants religious equality. Accordingly, it is not permissible to give preferential support and status to any church body, otherwise the principle of self-government, which the churches claim, would be jeopardized. Roman Catholics and Protestants may use the same nomenclature when discussing religious liberty, but the concepts may not be identical and this is understandable for each operates—philosophically and pragmatically, theologically and ecclesiologically—within a different framework. For example we may think of the ideologies represented by Thomas Aquinas and the Protestant concept of "the priesthood of believers," dealt with earlier. Consequently, from a Protestant viewpoint and that of the historical American concept of separation of church and state, much points in the direction that in theory and practice the Declaration of Religious Freedom is, or could become, another riddle of Roman Catholicism.

9

THE RELIGIOUS ROOTS AND PRINCIPLES OF AMERICAN DEMOCRACY

Enshrined in the national anthem of the United States of America is the phrase, "the land of the free and the home of the brave." The quest of the Pilgrim Fathers for freedom from persecution in England because of their religious convictions led them to found the first permanent settlement in the New World, on December 25, 1620. For the same reason, over the next two decades the Puritans and other English nonconformists established colonies in various parts of New England. Notable among these was Roger Williams—banished from Boston in 1636 because he "questioned the right of the civil authorities to legislate in matters of conscience"[1]—who founded the city of Providence in Rhode Island, which became the cradle of full civil and religious freedom.

The next two and a half centuries brought thousands in search of freedom from civil and religious oppression in Europe. Freedom was the keynote of the Declaration of Independence signed on July 4, 1776: "We hold these truths to be self-evident, that all men are created equal, that they are endowed by their Creator with certain unalienable Rights, that among these are Life, Liberty, and the pursuit of Happiness."[2] On May 14, 1787, the Constitutional Convention began drafting the Constitution of the United States, progenitor of all such documents and, for two hundred years, the most durable of them all. One of the objectives listed in its preamble is the desire to "secure the Blessings of Liberty to ourselves and our Posterity."[3] The American Constitution is a monument to, as well as a prescription for, civil and religious liberty.

147

The First Amendment to the Constitution specified that "Congress shall make no law respecting an establishment of religion, or prohibiting the free exercise thereof; or abridging the freedom of speech, or of the press; or the right of the people to peacably assemble, to petition the government for a redress of grievances."4 Freedom of religion is mentioned first, as the basis for all other freedoms.

In recent decades not a session of the Supreme Court has been without several appeals involving an interpretation of the "establishment" and "free exercise" clauses of the First Amendment. Their juridical history is a tale of continuing tension between them. By the "establishment of religion" those who framed the Constitution intended to rule out the idea of a state church—the legacy of both Roman Catholic and Reformation ideology—that is, according any church preferred status and public support. Government in the United States was to be perpetually blind to religious differences. The "free exercise" clause guaranteed the right of everyone to practice the religion of his choice. Together, these two phrases provided for a free church in a free state—a church without a pope and a state without a king. The endeavor of the Supreme Court to preserve the delicate balance between no "establishment" and "free exercise" has proved to be its finest balancing act.

The First Amendment to the Constitution was never intended to ignore God or to ostracize Him or the principles of the gospel from the United States, as some misguided libertarians of the present day would have us believe. American coins bear the inscription "In God we trust." The Great Seal of the United States of America pictures the eye of God watching over the building of the nation. Inscribed on the Liberty Bell are the words of Scripture, "Proclaim liberty throughout all the land unto all the inhabitants thereof" (Leviticus 25:10). The oath of allegiance to the flag incorporates the phrase "one nation, under God." Many of the founders of the nation were deeply religious and sought divine guidance in its founding.

The ardent devotion to liberty that inspired the great thinkers and leaders of the Republic two centuries ago brought forth many impassioned statements such as that of Patrick Henry before the Virginia House of Burgesses on March 23, 1775, "Give me liberty or give me death."5   Engraved in marble on the rotunda of the Jefferson Memorial beside the Tidal Basin in Washington, D.C., are his immortal words, "I have sworn upon the altar of God, eternal hostility against every form of tyranny over the mind of man."6 Author of the Declaration of Independence, Thomas Jefferson has been called the "firebrand of democracy."

Freedom has ever been the great magnet that draws oppressed peoples from around the world. For wave after wave of immigrants the Statue of Liberty at the gateway to New York harbor, with the inscription "LIBERTY" on its brow, has symbolized the American concept of freedom from all kinds of tyranny. We should not soon forget that this concept is rooted in the gospel of Jesus Christ who said, "If the Son makes you free, you will be free indeed" (John 8:36). Civil and religious liberty are the practical application of the two fundamental requirements of the gospel to society and government, and these principles—love for God and for one's fellowmen—found more perfect expression in the United States of America than ever before in history or anywhere else on earth.

American democracy with its numerous blessings has its religious origin in a specific Protestant tradition, one that opposed both papal supremacy and the reformers' alliance with the state and subservience to the monarch. Its history is closely related to the development of toleration and religious liberty and the resulting separation of church and state—an ideal that first became translated into reality in the United States of America. This, more than anything else, has made America a land of opportunity and contributed to its position as a great champion of human rights in the world today and defender of democratic principles against all forces of tyranny.

For the same reason America has the richest church life of any nation. Without any Sunday laws it has a much larger church attendance than any nation in Europe. Without state support it maintains a well educated clergy, fine church buildings, excellent church-related schools, many active charitable church organizations, and a foreign missions program second to none.

Freedom is a tender plant that still requires tender, loving care, and only as we understand the historical process that made it possible and the formidable forces that, even today, threaten to deprive us of it, will we be able to preserve it for ourselves and for future generations. Today we tend to take freedom more or less for granted, as if it were as natural as the air we breathe. But the spirit of coercion and oppression is alive and flourishing in many parts of the world, and we are naive if we think ourselves immune to it. Although persecution is out of style, the basic concepts and claims that led to persecution in the past would revive with any attempt to change the present relationship between church and state. The same causes would lead to the same results. Democracy is rooted in religious freedom and can continue to exist only where there is true religious freedom as well. This chapter explores the historical roots of freedom and democracy and contemporary issues that threaten it.

TOLERATION AND LIBERTY

The various acts of toleration enacted in Europe differ greatly from the principle of religious liberty: "The one is a concession, the other a right; the one is a matter of expediency, the other a principle; the one is a gift of man, the other a gift of God."7

Religious persecution usually arose from some form of union between church and state. A relaxation of the relationship between church and state results in toleration, but only when there is absolute separation between church and state can there be religious liberty. This became the case in the founding of the United States of America, where the ideal of a free church in a free state was first realized; likewise, the principle that self-support and self-government are inseparable. In the American Constitution—a Magna Charta of religious liberty—a New Testament principle and a sixteenth century ideal became a reality. Summarizing the progress of religious liberty, Philip Schaff makes the following apt evaluation:

The history of religious liberty teaches important lessons. Intolerance and persecution have wrought incalculable misery in the past, and are contrary to the spirit of Christianity, justice, and mercy, and incompatible with modern civilization; while liberty has proved to be the best friend of religion, and receives from it its strongest moral support. Spiritual offences should be spiritually judged and punished according to the gospel; temporal offences should be temporally judged and punished according to the law. The best legal guarantee of religious liberty is a peaceful separation of the spiritual and temporal power; the best moral guarantee of liberty is human culture and Christian charity.

The Church needs and should ask nothing from the State but the protection of law. She commends herself best to the world by attending to her proper spiritual duties and keeping aloof from political and secular complications. She can only lose by force and violence; she can only gain and succeed by the spiritual weapons of truth and love.[8]

The growth of toleration, a loosening of the relationship between church and state and eventually the absolute separation of church and state, and the realization of religious liberty as seen in the United States of America, are all closely related to the development of modern democracy.

MODERN DEMOCRACY
AND THE RADICAL REFORMATION

It is widely recognized that the Protestant doctrine of the "priesthood of all believers" made the Reformation the starting point of modern democratic ideas. But the development of democratic principles took place in a particular branch of the Protestant movement—among the Baptists, the Independents or Congregationalists, and the Puritans. In his outstanding work, *The Modern Democratic State,* A.D. Lindsay writes:

The most significant thing about Puritan democratic theory is that the Puritans began with the experience of working a small and thoroughly democratic society, the Puritan congregation. Their idea of a church is that it is a fellowship of active believers. The

Puritans of the Left, with whom democratic theories mostly originated, were all congregationalists—to use the later term. The self-governing congregation was for them the church. In such a society all are equal, in the sense, as we have seen, that they were all equally called of God.

That fundamental fact outweighed their differences of ability, capacity, character, and wealth so completely that these differences could be freely recognized and made use of.... Their genuine experienced democracy was not political, but the democracy of a voluntary society—a society which did not use force in the putting into practice of its decision, but was a fellowship of discussion.... The practice and organization of the Society of Friends works out most completely the logic of this democratic experience, with its assumptions that all members alike may have something to enlighten the others; that if men and women meet together in the right spirit, something new and profound comes out of the discussions.... Because the Puritan tradition started with the experience of a society which rested on consent and abjured the use of force, it tended to conceive the state on the analogy of such a society.9

A. D. Lindsay states further, "It is clear how much of the operative ideals of English and American democracy follows this pattern: the belief in the all-importance of the free associations in tolerance and diversity: in the instrumental and secondary function of the state: in the depreciation of force and the exaltation of the voluntary principle."10 The voice of the people, as expressed by each member of each congregation, thus exerted great influence upon the formation of modern democratic theories.

Early Reformation history points also to the fact that, to a large degree, modern democracy originated among the Baptists, especially the Dutch Baptists and their associates in England who followed them years later. The Lutheran and English Reformation expressed itself politically by confirming the absolute power of the monarchy. The Baptists, on the other hand, were opposed by the major churches when they advocated freedom of conscience and the free church principle. In his monumental work *The Social Teaching of the Christian Churches,* Ernst Troeltsch points out that the concept of freedom of conscience and toleration, so basic for democracy, was a "logical result of the rise of Congregationalism and the Free Church Movement."11 To this historical fact we will now turn.

The persecuted Baptists found a haven of refuge in the Netherlands. In this small country, which threw off the yoke of Spanish absolutism, the ideal of representative government was of ancient origin. It is significant that out of its system of representative government grew high social standards. The toleration and freedom of the Dutch "became the envy of the whole world." In his book *Christianity and Politics*, Albert Hyma emphasizes the religious source for this development:

> Even more influential and effective than the age-old feudal contracts in the Netherlands was the powerful leaven of the newly born Baptist Church, which developed so rapidly in the northern Netherlands that the period from 1530 to 1566 is not dominated by Lutheranism or Calvinism, but by a religious movement that had been born upon Dutch soil, namely the *Devotio Moderna....* Inasmuch as the Reformation in the Netherlands from 1530 to 1566 is known to have been practically nothing else than the history of the Baptist churches in that country, the significance of this movement is apparent. Modern democracy, as has often been pointed out...has in a large degree sprung from the labors of the Dutch Baptists and their associates in England, who followed them much later.12

In 1572 William of Orange granted the Baptists of Holland religious freedom and toleration. The political theories of the Baptists in the Netherlands became the heritage of Baptists in England, where the first Baptist church was established in London in 1611 or 1612. During the persecution of dissenters in England many fled to the Netherlands where they found a haven of refuge. These refugees, whether Independents or Calvinists, were strongly influenced by the democratic principles of the Baptists and the Dutch people, and for a time Cromwell considered uniting his own Puritan commonwealth with that of the Dutch. It is therefore not surprising that the inner religious struggle in England, lasting for about 150 years from Henry VIII to James II, ended in the Act of Toleration of 1689, which William of Orange issued soon after he became king of England.

The Independents and the Baptists strongly influenced such men as John Locke and John Milton, who were energetic defenders of freedom of conscience. The Pilgrim Fathers, who crossed the Atlantic in the Mayflower in 1620, founded the colony of Plymouth and thus planted Congregationalism in New England. Roger Williams—a Baptist—introduced full religious freedom in Rhode Island in 1636. The closing words of the charter, signed by the first settlers in Providence, states that "all men may walk as their consciences persuade them, every one in the name of his God."13 Under the leadership of William Penn the Quakers carried the same principle to Pennsylvania. The first Germans who chose America as a new country were thirty Mennonite families who came to America in 1683.

The story of the American forefathers testifies to the religious origin of American democracy and to the fact that the basic principle of this democracy has its roots in the "sects" of the Reformation period—the Baptists, Congregationalists, Presbyterians, Unitarians, Quakers, and other evangelical movements of the eighteenth and nineteenth centuries. James H. Nichols refers to the fact that many Americans have "been quite unaware of the fact that the moral dynamic of their democracy was the creation of one very specific Protestant ethical tradition, and that, with a few minor exceptions, it was the peculiar product of that single tradition."14 As Nichols points out, that single tradition is Puritan Protestantism:

> Puritanism alone, and especially Congregationalism, Presbyterianism, and the Baptists, supplied the colonists with a consistent and unembarrassed

democratic political ethic,...the primary motive of
Puritan democracy was liberty for the fulfillment of
religious responsibility, liberty both in the State and
against the State.... Puritan democracy, functioning
by free discussion, values and protects minorities
and "the opposition."...Puritan Protestantism, whatever its other failings, had humanized and moralized
politics in absolute superiority to every other
Christian tradition. And it had done so on the program of liberal democracy.15

POLITICAL AND RELIGIOUS FREEDOM

In the history of toleration and freedom we find that the
claim for religious liberty has often opened the door for political and
social freedom. In this connection it is of interest to notice that in a
major study of religious liberty M. Searle Bates observed that
"International law and religious liberty grew in intimate association."16 We will also find that where religious liberty is denied or
only toleration granted, political and social freedom is missing and
as a consequence progress is hampered.

It is in the creation of man as the image of God that we find
the basic and distinct rationale for the recognition and preservation
of human rights. Thomas Paine recognized this in his renowned
book *The Rights of Man* (1791), in which he defended the constitutional attempts of France and America to guarantee human
rights. Wrote Paine:

The error of those who reason by precedents drawn
from antiquity, respecting the rights of man, is, that
they do not go far enough into antiquity. They do
not go the whole way. They stop in some of the intermediate stages of an hundred or a thousand years,
...but if we proceed on, we shall at last come out
right: we shall come to the time when man came
from the hand of his maker. What was he then?
Man. Man was his high and only title, and a higher
cannot be given him.17

Thomas Jefferson drafted the Declaration of Independence (1776) in which it was affirmed as "self-evident" that "all men are created equal and that they are endowed by their Creator with certain unalienable Rights."

While the total biblical concept of freedom was not conceived and realize in the social and political sphere, there has through the centuries been a growing awareness of individual freedom as part of humanness. At the close of the Second World War, Franklin D. Roosevelt stated his famous four freedoms in an address to the United States Congress. They were: "freedom of speech and expression—everywhere in the world.... the freedom of every person to worship God in his own way—everywhere in the world.... freedom from want... everywhere in the world... [and] freedom from fear... anywhere in the world"18

In the preamble to the Universal Declaration of Human Rights, proclaimed by the General Assembly of the United Nations (1948) recognition was made "of the inherent dignity and of the equal and inalienable rights of all members of the human family" as "the foundation of freedom, justice and peace in the world." Accordingly, Article 1 reads: "All human beings are born free and equal in dignity and rights. They are endowed with reason and conscience and should act towards one another in a spirit of brotherhood." Article 18 provides that "everyone has the right to freedom of thought, conscience and religion; this right includes freedom to change his religion or belief, and freedom, either alone or in community with others and in public or private, to manifest his religion or belief in teaching, practice, worship and observance."19

The Second World Congress on Religious Liberty (sponsored by the International Religious Liberty Association and others) had as its theme, "Freedom of Religion and Belief: Basis of Peace." The congress, held in Rome in September 1984, and attended by representatives from the major religions and various political systems who affirmed the theme of the conference. The secretary-general of the International Religious Liberty Association, Dr. Bert Beverly Beach, stated in his welcome and opening remarks:

> I want freedom for the Christian, Jew, Muslim, Buddhist and Hindu, old and new religions, for the

Marxist and non-Marxist, for the believer and what
we call the nonbeliever, for the religious or ideological majority and for the minority. I'll tell you one
important reason why: my freedom of conscience
and belief is never secure, if your freedom is not secure. I must even guard the freedom of belief of one
who might style himself my ideological adversary.
Let men travel to their ultimate destiny in freedom
and good conscience. Really, freedom of religion
allows of no other travel. The spirit of this
Conference is epitomized in the Golden Rule, which
is the concluding statement of the IRLA Declaration
of Principles: "Do unto others as you would have
others do unto you."[20]

Similar thoughts were expressed by Abraham Lincoln when
he wrote to H. L. Pierce in 1859: "Those who deny freedom to
others desire it not for themselves,"[21] and by Thomas Paine in
1776: "Those who expect to reap the blessings of freedom must,
like men, undergo the fatigue of supporting it."[22]

A FREE CHURCH IN A FREE STATE

The principle of a free church in a free state was first realized
in the United States and accounts for its prosperity both in church
and state. It also testifies to the blessing that results from Christ's
words "Render unto Caesar the things that are Caesar's, and unto
God the things that are God's." The progress of democracy in other
countries, together with the prosperity of church and state, appear to
be in equal proportion to the extent that the ideals of Puritan Protestantism are recognized. Similar efforts to establish a fruitful democracy in countries that do not have this heritage have failed, or are
failing.

The religious beginnings and historical development of
modern democracy constitute a serious warning to present-day
democracy. It is evident that true democracy can only be preserved
when a free church exists in a free state, each discharging its own
responsibility. This freedom is in danger from the influence of both

political and religious authoritarianism. For all who love freedom the following statement can be a watchword for the present and the future: "Whatever temporary alliances might be expedient, Puritan Protestantism was responsible to God alone and could yield its conscience to no infallible interpreters—neither to a party nor to a hierarchy."[23]

While there are nuances in the interpretation of the historical events and issues we have observed, and variations are to be found in the application of these ideological concepts, the fact remains that in the political and religious arena two developments have confronted each other. One of these is represented by papal supremacy, with all of its religious and political implications, and the other by anti-papal movements whether religiously or politically motivated. This development, which led to the American ideological separation of church and state, is fundamental to the whole of the American society. At the same time, however, the century-old conflict is still with us. In his comment on the canon dealing with the jurisdiction and supremacy of the pope in the Canon Law of 1917, Chas. Augustine, O.S.B., observed that "all those who pervert the essential divine organization of the Church as a perfect society of the monarchical type, necessarily deny the power of the Roman Pontiff."[24]   Neither did the 1984 revision of Canon Law alter the monarchical structure of the church, nor did it redefine the authority of the pope.

Proclaiming "errors about civil society, considered both in itself and in its relation to the Church," the papal Syllabus of Errors (1864) listed as an error the idea that "The Church ought to be separated from the State, and the State from the Church,"[25] a reference which would include the United States of America. While this "error" has been modified, the undergirding philosophy is the same. In this connection it is worthwhile to notice Professor Emerton's closing statement in his book on Marsilius: "Certainly American democracy, if it is to work out the mission with which it seems to be entrusted, cannot afford to refuse the support or to neglect the warnings it may derive from a study of Marsiglio's ardent plea for a Peace of the world...."[26]

The role of Thomas Aquinas in the formulation of Catholic theology and its bearing on the issue under discussion has already been noted. The medieval controversy over "realism" and "nominalism" and its bearing upon the value of the individual as the source of power, both in church and society, is with us today and must be recognized.

The late Cardinal Bea, who became the first director of the Secretariat for the Promotion of the Unity of Christians at the time of the second Vatican Council, perceived the Protestant concept under discussion and at the same time underscored the great difference between Protestantism and Catholicism on this point, both in the past and in the present. Wrote Bea:

> In days gone by, Protestantism, especially in its Lutheran form, had a distinctly individualistic character.... He [man] was to live in God's sight quite simply, reading and interpreting the Bible under the guidance of the Holy Spirit, who enlightened him and directed his life.... [Roman Catholicism] places them [the doctrines] in the great current of tradition. Fundamentally it is the method of the Catholic Church, which is anti-individualist.... The whole Reformation world rejected in principle any authority in the Church which could oblige the consciences of the faithful to follow it. From this stems a very practical obstacle to all efforts at unity.[27]

Commenting on the responsibility of every individual to study the Bible for himself Dean Farrar wrote: "According to the Reformers each Christian has not only the privilege but also the duty to examine and judge Christian beliefs and practises on the basis of the Bible. Wrote Luther: 'To ascertain and judge about doctrine pertains to all and every Christian; and in such a way that let him be anathema who injures their right by a single hair.'"[28]

THE AMERICAN RELIGIOUS LANDSCAPE

When, today, we look at the political and religious landscape of America as it relates to the topic under discussion, the appointment of an ambassador to the Holy See is only the tip of the iceberg.

Ideological changes are taking place in all areas of life, but before new norms replace old constitutional principles it is of vital necessity to ask what, historically, made America the society it has been, for without doubt only that which made America can preserve it.

The arena in which fundamental and constitutional principles are formulated and promulgated is that of religious faith, and especially how that faith relates itself to the secular order. It may be of value to take note of the composition of American churches.

Due to immigration and a higher birthrate among Roman Catholics there has been a continual increase in church-affiliated Catholics. In 1940 its membership stood at a little more than twenty-one million, whereas by 1984 it had passed the fifty-two million mark. That same year the membership of the Protestant churches was nearly seventy-nine million. The family of Baptist churches forms the largest Protestant group, with the Southern Baptist Convention having a membership of fourteen million (1984). The majority of Methodists belong to the United Methodist Church, with the second largest membership of nine million (1982). Then follow the Presbyterian Church (U.S.A.), three million (1984); and the Evangelical Lutheran Church in America and the Lutheran Church-Missouri Synod with about eight million members between them, and the United Presbyterian Church and the Episcopal Church with about three million members each. The Protestant membership of one hundred eighty-six churches constitutes the Christian majority in America, but while Roman Catholic membership has increased, Protestant membership has decreased from sixty-five percent of the population in 1900 to about forty six percent in 1970.29

Among American Protestants, especially since Vatican II, anti-Catholic sentiment has largely disappeared, but without coming to grips with fundamental theological issues. The latter may be considered the weakness of present-day Protestant ecumenism in its dialogue with Roman Catholicism. At the same time the trend of American Protestantism has been "described as transformationist with regard to church-state relations. This position applies a theocratic principle (the sovereignty of God) to church-state theory and practice, and is committed to a prophetic church, a strong social ethic and a realistic view of sin."30

It is obvious that the American denominational spectrum includes variations of faith and practice, but at each end of the spectrum are opposing concepts. Historically the one is represented by papal supremacy within Roman Catholicism, and the other by Puritan Protestantism, or the Free Church principle, especially among the Baptists, Methodists, Presbyterians, and others.

The American people are known for their pragmatism, a trait also reflected in their religious life. It is one of their strengths, but it can also become a weakness. The administration of a church should follow different norms from temporal society and secular organizations. While the Protestant decision-making process should include dialogue and consensus, it should not be guided by a popularity poll. Plans and decisions must take place within an authentic biblical, theological, spiritual, and religious framework.

If there is a weakness in American Protestantism it is the lack of historical depth, a fact which is generally true of the nation at large, not having centuries of history behind it. Historical insight creates conviction. If Protestantism lacks conviction, the reason may be a certain negligence or lack of appreciation of a common historical heritage among the one hundred eighty-six Protestant denominations representing seventy-eight million Christians, compared with one Roman Catholic Church with fifty-two million members.

American materialism has led the nation into a moral vacuum which portends frightening results for society. Moral values are rooted in the Christian religion because they stem from the character of God. Moral values cannot be separated from the revealed truths of the Bible and an honest adherence to them. The quest must therefore be for authentic biblical truth regarding God's plan for the individual, and for the present and future destiny of planet earth. Thus the blueprint to be sought is not Roman, nor American, nor can any crusade be Roman-American! What must be proclaimed is a biblical message with evangelical zeal, dynamic conviction, and prophetic insight rooted in the gospel of Jesus Christ. The religious heritage of America tells us that this can best be accomplished by a free church in a free state, where no single religious entity has a preferential status.

10

POSTSCRIPT:
The Eschatological Dimension

The Christian evaluation of the conditions, meaning, and purpose of life is conceived within the framework of a great conflict between good and evil. This controversy, with its theological issues, is centered in three great events: (1) the primeval temptation and fall of man; (2) the incarnation of Christ, with correlative events of the crucifixion, the resurrection, and the ascension; and (3) the second advent of Christ. God's promise of redemption following the original fall of man, the redemptive effects of the incarnation of Christ, and the assurance of the glorification of the saved at His second coming, together with the Edenic restoration of the earth, make the message of the Bible one of hope.

In the ancient world man had little concept of history. He understood history merely as a circular repetition of events. The uniqueness of the Hebrew prophets' concept of history was linear, climaxing in the appearance of the Son of man.

In the same painting a landscape painter may portray a village, with its houses and people in the foreground, and in the background a valley and hills, sky and sun, even though some are a very great distance away. In their description of the future the Bible writers likewise depict the first and second advents of Christ, the first in the foreground and the latter in the background of salvation history.

The many-faceted biblical hope does not move in a circle, with one center, around the first or the second advents of Christ; it moves as in an ellipse, which has two foci, around both events, inseparably. The New Testament writers expressed strong faith in a fully realized hope at the second advent as the climactic result of the redemptive accomplishments of Christ's first advent.

At the Fall of man the door to heaven closed, with God as it were inside and man outside. The incarnation of Christ with the correlative events of the crucifixion, the resurrection, and the ascension opened the door to heaven, with God still inside and man outside. But those events gave us a future and a hope. The historical division of time into years, "B.C." and "A.D.," has greater significance than a mere calendar reveals; it reminds us that Christ is the pivot of history, and that at the second advent man will enter through the opened door and forever remain with God. World history and salvation history constantly move toward this point.

The early Christians were conscious of living through the turning point of the great controversy between good and evil. Christ's crucifixion, resurrection, and ascension had already set in motion a change in the order of this world. Through the opened door the Holy Spirit descended and empowered the early Christians with a new life they could not have obtained by themselves, and that power was to remain with them until the end. Though they realized that the transition was well under way, they also realized that it would not reach completion this side of the second advent. The apostle John said: "Beloved, we are God's children now; it does not yet appear what we shall be, but we know that when He appears we shall be like him, for we shall see Him as He is" (1 John 3:2). To the Christian the time between the two advents is one of a certain tension between "we are God's children now" and "it does not yet appear what we shall be." This tension cannot be eliminated, and Christian historical realism advises us that the present and the future must be seen and lived in the light of this polarity. The "now" and the "not yet" can be illustrated from an experience of the second World War.

When the Allied forces landed in Normandy and secured a strong foothold on the continent, the war was not won, but the decisive battle had been won. We refer to that event as D-day. The first advent of Christ was the D-day, and the second advent will be the V-day in the battle between God and his foes. History as we experience it should be regarded as an interim between the disclosure of God in Jesus Christ in the first advent—"We have beheld

His glory, glory as of the only Son from the Father" (John 1:14)—
and the fulfillment of its meaning at the second advent, which is
both the end and goal of the "present age." When the Book of
Revelation speaks about God as "the Alpha and Omega, the beginning and the end" (Rev. 21:6), the word "end" (in the Greek, *telos*)
means full performance, perfect discharge, final dealing, fulfillment,
realization, ultimate destiny. By divine judgment of both human and
cosmic powers an end will be brought to sin and thereby to the
pride, self-centeredness, corruption, and incompleteness of human
history. At the same time the goal of history will be reached when
"God has put all things in subjection under his feet.... then the Son
himself will also be subjected to him who put all things under him,
that God may be everything to everyone (1 Cor. 15:25, 28).

Church history tells us that, to a large degree, Christian doctrines and practices have focused upon either the first advent or the
second advent. The former has been the inclination by established
churches, the latter by apocalyptic movements. Each advent is a
distinct event, to be sure, but the message or truth of each should be
seen in totality, both in doctrinal teaching and in the pragmatic life of
the individual and the church. The two advents should also serve as
a helpful guide or tuning fork in understanding the church's activities and its relation to society and the world at large. The Christian
lives in the world but is "not of the world" (John 17:14). His
Christian realism regarding a sinful world tells him not to hope for a
lasting peace apart from the second advent. Only in the correlation
of the two advents can the Christian hope, promises, and redemptive
activities be fulfilled, partly in this present life and completely in the
everlasting kingdom of God. The first advent made the second advent possible, but what the first advent gained, can only be realized
fully at the second advent.

In man's view of the future the pendulum has generally
swung between optimism and pessimism. The first has its source in
the original divine design for man and is renewed in the belief in the
kingdom of God; the latter originated in the fall of man and continued because of his sinfulness. The Christian view of the future is
one of biblical realism. Having experienced the power of the Holy
Spirit, the Christian is not a hopeless pessimist. But also realizing
the demonic power of sin in the present age the Christian is not un-

duly or naively optimistic either. Christ said, "My kingship is not of this world" (John 18:36). Christian optimism is anchored in the inseparability of the two advents of Christ. The closing words of the Bible: "Come, Lord Jesus" (Rev. 22:20), echo the prayer of both the Old and the New Testament.

Generally speaking the Roman Catholic Church perceives its mission for the world uneschatologically. To a large degree the same may be said of the World Council of Churches. The trend within Roman Catholicism and much of Protestantism is to humanize and naturalize biblical eschatology, and then, with an uneschatological gospel, to transform the present world into the "Celestial City" of God. In this process the principles guarding the American concept of separation of church and state will be undermined.

The moral leadership of the pope is to be respected and may be applauded by Christians at large, and it is right to recognize that the first advent of Christ empowered the Christian community to exemplify the principles of the kingdom of God. But we must also recognize that, without the prospect of a literal second advent of Christ, the hope for lasting peace and justice would be false, anti-biblical, and unchristian.

The realism of biblical eschatology must have its rightful place. For many it was regrettable that the Pope John XXIII in his opening speech at Vatican Council II said: "We feel we must disagree with those prophets of gloom, who are always forecasting disaster, as though the end of the world were at hand."[1] Many Bible-oriented Christians believe "the signs of the time" tell us that Christ's second advent is near. "Be ye also ready" should be the watchword for the Christian church.

At his first advent Jesus was rejected by his people and its leaders because they had hoped for a Messiah who would give them political freedom from Rome and establish their nation as the kingdom of God. It has always been difficult for sinful man to distinguish between spiritual realities and temporal goals. In his great discourse on watching for the signs of the times, Christ compared the time of the end with that of the destruction of Jerusalem, where incompatible religious-political ambitions and goals were buried under the ruins of the city.

Scripture perceives history as linear and as climaxing in a specific historical event—the appearance of the Son of man and the establishment of the kingdom of God. Having seen in vision the succession of the world powers, the prophet Daniel describes the goal of history in these words:

> I saw in the night visions, and behold, with the clouds of heaven there came one like a Son of Man, and he came to the Ancient of Days and was presented before him. And to Him was given dominion, glory and a kingdom, that all peoples, nations, and languages should serve Him; his dominion is an everlasting dominion, which shall not pass away and His kingdom one which shall not be destroyed (Dan. 7:13-14, N.A.S.B.).

Jesus not only took the title "Son of Man" from the Book of Daniel, but lived the vision as He proclaimed the kingdom of God. He knew His role in the great drama of history pictured by Daniel, as did the apostles and the early church.

The Christian is called to represent the spiritual realities of the kingdom of God, but not to transform this present world into the "new earth." The great conflict between good and evil will continue until the end. Christ said, "The ruler of this world is coming. He has no power over me" (John 14:30). At His second advent Christ himself will create a new earth and world order for those who, by the Holy Spirit, have been "born again" into the kingdom of heaven.

In the face of man's ability to destroy himself and his world because of the moral "cancer" at work in his creative activities, the doctrine of the second advent of Christ becomes the hope, the assurance, and the affirmation that ultimately the purpose of God for planet earth will prevail. The guarantee of fulfillment is found in the Christian faith aligned to the redemptive historical events of the first advent. "God has allowed us to know the secret of his plan, and it is this: he purposed long ago in his sovereign will that all human history should be consummated in Christ, that everything that exists in Heaven or earth should find its perfection and fulfillment in Him" (Eph. 1:10, Phillips Translation).

NOTES

CHAPTER ONE

PAPAL SUPREMACY, JURISDICTION, AND INFALLIBILITY: Its Beginnings and Development

1. Jaroslav Pelikan, *The Riddle of Roman Catholicism* (New York: Abingdon Press, 1959), p. 10.

2. Jean Guitton, in B. B. Beach, *Vatican II: Bridging the Abyss* (Washington, D.C.: Review and Herald Publishing Association, 1968), p. 305.

3. W. J. Sparrow Simpson, *Roman Catholic Opposition to Papal Infallibility* (Milwaukee, Wisconsin: The Young Churchman Company, 1910), p. 273.

4. Philip Schaff, *The Creeds of Christendom, vol. II, The Greek and Latin Creeds* (New York: Harper & Brothers, 1877), pp. 234, 259-265, passim.

5. Schaff, p. 212.

6. Schaff, pp. 270-271.

7. Hans Leitzmann, *The Beginnings of the Christian Church* (London: Camelot Press, 1937), pp. 111, 132.

8. Oscar Cullman, *Peter: Disciple, Apostle, Martyr* (New York: Meridian Books, 1958), p. 116.

9. H. Burn-Murdoch, *The Development of the Papacy* (London: Faber and Faber Limited, n.d.), p. 72.

10. Ludwig Schopp, ed., *The Fathers of the Church*, vol. 1, *The Apostolic Fathers* (Washington, D.C.: The Catholic University of America Press, 1962), p. 109.

11. W. S. Kerr, *A Handbook on the Papacy* (London: Marshall, Morgan, and Scott, 1950) p. 70.

12. Kirsopp Lake, *Eusebius, the Ecclesiastical History* (Cambridge, Massachusetts: Harvard University Press, 1926), vol. I, p. 183.

13. Alexander Roberts and James Donaldson, eds., *The Ante-Nicene Fathers*, vol. 1, *The Apostolic Fathers* (Grand Rapids, Michigan: Wm. B. Eerdmans Publishing Company, 1956), pp. 414-415.

14. Henry Bettenson, selector and ed., *Documents of the Christian Church* (London: Oxford University Press, 1943), p. 116.

15. Philip Schaff and Henry Wace, *A Select Library of Nicene and Post-Nicene Fathers of the Christian Church*, vol. I, *Eusebius* (New York: The Christian Literature Company, 1890), p. 241, note 1.

16. Schaff and Wace, p. 243.

17. J. N. D. Kelly, *The Oxford Dictionary of Popes* (New York: Oxford University Press, 1986), p. 6.

18. Williston Walker, *A History of the Christian Church* (New York: Charles Scribner's Sons, 1959), p. 67.

19. Schaff and Wace, p. 316.

20. A. B. Hasler, *How the Pope Became Infallible* (Garden City, New York: Doubleday and Company, Inc., 1981), p. 34.

21. Hasler, p. 35.

22. Hasler.

23. C. J. Hefele, *A History of the Councils of the Church* (Edinburgh: T. and T. Clark, 1876), vol. 2, p. 69.

24. H. Burn-Murdoch, p. 213.

25. Burn-Murdoch, p. 213.

26. J. W. C. Wand, *A History of the Early Church to A.D. 500* (London: Methuen and Company, Ltd., 1937), p. 237.

27. Philip Schaff and Henry Wace, eds., *A Select Library of Nicene and Post-Nicene Fathers of the Christian Church*, vol. XII, *Leo the Great and Gregory the Great* (Grand Rapids, Michigan: Wm. B. Eerdmans Publishing Company, 1956), p. 117.

28. Schaff and Wace, p. 291.

29. Schaff and Wace, p. 195.

30. Philip Schaff, *History of the Christian Church, vol. IV, Mediaeval Christianity* (Grand Rapids, Michigan: Wm. B. Eerdmans Publishing Company, 1957), p. 212.

31. A. C. Flick, *The Rise of the Mediaeval Church* (New York: Burt Franklin, 1909), p. 191.

32. Horace K. Mann, *The Lives of the Popes in the Early Middle Ages* (London: Kegan Paul, Trench, Trubner and Company, Ltd., 1925), vol. III, pp. 46, 52.

33. Mann., p. 59.

34. Mann., p. 75.

35. Ernest F. Henderson, trans. and ed., *Select Historical Documents of the Middle Ages* (London: George Bell and Sons, Ltd., 1905), pp. 366-367.

36. M. Deansley, *A History of the Medieval Church, 590-1500* (London: Methuen and Company, Ltd., 1925), p. 143.

37. H. Burn-Murdoch, pp. 76-77.

38. Schaff, vol. V, *The Middle Ages, 1049-1294,* p. 157.

39. O. J. Thatcher and E. H. McNeal, *A Source Book for Medieval History* (New York: Charles Scribner's Sons, 1905), pp. 315.

40. Thatcher and McNeal, pp. 314-317.

41. Schaff, vol. VI, *The Middle Ages, 1294-1517,* p. 25.

CHAPTER TWO

ROME'S INTERNAL CONFLICT

1. Alexander C. Flick, *The Decline of the Medieval Church* (London: Kegan Paul, Trench, Trubner and Company, Ltd., 1930), p. 460.

2. Henry Bettenson, ed., *Documents of the Christian Church* (London: Oxford University Press, 1943), pp. 192, 193.

3. Philip Hughes, *A History of the Church* (New York: Sheed and Ward, 1934), vol. 3, pp. 298, 299.

4. William Shan Kerr, *A Handbook of the Papacy* (London: Marshall, Morgan and Scott, 1950), p. 261.

5. Philip Schaff, *History of the Christian Church,* vol. VI, *The Middle Ages, 1294-1517* (Grand Rapids, Michigan: Wm. B. Eerdmans Publishing Company, 1957), p. 170.

6. Schaff, p. 172.

7. Williston Walker, *A History of the Christian Church* (New York: Charles Scribner's Sons, 1959), p. 279.

8. Thomas A. Lindsay, *A History of the Reformation* (Edinburgh: T. and T. Clark, 1908), vol. II, p. 590.

9. Lindsay, p. 593.

10. Philip Schaff, *The Creeds of Christendom,* vol. II, *The Greek and Latin Creeds* (New York: Harper & Brothers, 1877), pp. 209, 210.

11. Martin E. Marty, *A Short History of Christianity* (Philadelphia: Fortress Press, 1980), p. 278.

12. Schaff, p. 222.

13. George Salmon, *The Infallibility of the Church* (Grand Rapids, Michigan: Baker Book House, 1959), p. 323.

14. August Bernhard Hasler, *How the Pope Became Infallible* (Garden City, New York: Doubleday and Company, Inc., 1981), pp. 53, 57-58.

15. Schaff, vol. I, *The History of the Creeds*, p. 144.

16. Schaff, vol. II, p. 77.

17. Schaff, p. 234.

18. Schaff, vol. I, p. 144.

19. Schaff, p. 155.

20. Schaff, pp. 157-158.

21. Schaff, p. 162.

22. Johann Ignaz von Döllinger, *Declarations and Letters on the Vatican Decrees* (Edinburgh: T. and T. Clark, 1891), p. 30.

23. Döllenger, p. 103.

CHAPTER THREE

A CHURCH WITH A SOVEREIGN STATE AND SECULAR POWER

1. Christopher Dawson, *The Making of Europe* (London: Sheed and Ward, 1932), pp. 27-28.

2. Dawson, p. 29.

3. John P. McKnight, *The Papacy, A New Appraisal* (New York: Rinehart and Company, Inc., 1952), p. 181.

4. Dawson, p. 153.

5. H. H. Milman, *History of Latin Christianity* (New York: John Murray, 1854), vol. 2, book 3, p. 73.

6. Philip Schaff, *History of the Christian Church, vol. IV, Mediaeval Christianity* (Grand Rapids, Michigan: Wm. B. Eerdmans Publishing Company, 1957), p. 98.

7. Otto Gierke, *Political Theories of the Middle Age* (Boston: Beacon Press, 1958), p. 9.

8. Gierke, p. 10.

9. Thomas M. Parker, *Christianity and the State in the Light of History* (London: Harper and Brothers, 1955), p. 110.

10. Parker, p. 111.

11. Gierke, pp. 11-12.

12. John N. Figgis, *From Gerson to Grotius* (Cambridge: The University Press, 1956), p. 4.

13. George A. Campbell, *The Crusades* (London: Duckworth, 1935), p. 45.

14. James Bryce, *The Holy Roman Empire* (Boston: Estes and Lauriat, n.d.), p. 175.

15. Bryce, p. 59.

16. Louis Duchesne, trans. A. H. Matthew, *The Beginnings of the Temporal Sovereignty of the Popes, A.D. 754-1073* (London: Kegan Paul, Trench, Trubner and Company, Ltd., 1908), p. 119.

17. Schaff, p. 252.

18. Horace K. Mann, *The Lives of the Popes in the Early Middle Ages* (London: Kegan Paul, Trench, Trubner and Company, Ltd., 1925), vol. I, part II, p. 309.

19. Schaff, pp. 234-235.

20. H. M. Gwatkin and J. P. Whitney, eds., *The Cambridge Medieval History* (Cambridge: The University Press, 1926), vol. II, p. 586.

21. Duchesne, p. 120.

22. Walter Ullmann, *The Growth of Papal Government in the Middle Ages* (New York: Barnes and Noble, Inc., 1955), p. 75.

23. Ullmann, p. 78.

24. Ernest F. Henderson, trans. and ed., *Select Historical Documents of the Middle Ages* (London: George Bell and Sons, Ltd., 1905), pp. 319-329, passim.

25. Bryce, p. 96.

26. Schaff, p. 273.

27. Mann, vol. III, pp. 46, 52.

28. Mann, p. 59.

29. Mann, p. 70.

30. Mann, p. 75.

31. Schaff, pp. 276-277; see also Mann, pp. 83-96.

32. Alexander C. Flick, *The Rise of the Mediaeval Church* (New York: Burt Franklin Press, 1909), p. 344.

33. Duchesne, p. 224.

34. Bryce, p. 135.

35. Geddes MacGregor, *The Vatican Revolution* (Boston: Beacon Press, 1957), p. 102.

36. Thomas Greenwood, Cathedra Petri: *A Political History of the Great Latin Patriarchate* (London: C. J. Stewart, 1856), book X, chap. VI, p. 286.

37. Greenwood, p. 298.

38. Henry Bettenson, *Documents of the Christian Church* (New York: Oxford University Press, 1943), pp. 157-158.

39. Bettenson, p. 158.

40. Flick, *The Rise of the Mediaeval Church,* p. 450.

41. Bryce, pp. 178, 179.

42. Alexander C. Flick, *The Decline of the Medieval Church* (New York: Burt Franklin, 1930), pp. 5-6.

43. G. G. Coulton, *Five Centuries of Religion* (Cambridge: The University Press, 1950), vol. 2, p. 18.

CHAPTER FOUR

VATICAN DIPLOMACY

1.   Robert A. Graham, *Vatican Diplomacy* (Princeton: Princeton University Press, 1959), p. 182.

2.   Hans Küng, trans. Eric Mosbacher, *Infallible? An Enquiry* (Glasglow: William Collins Sons and Company, Ltd., Fount Paperbacks, 1980), p. 75.

3.   Graham, pp. 181-182.

4.   L. Barbarito, "Vatican City, State of," *New Catholic Encyclopedia*, vol. 14, p. 557.

5.   Graham, p. 183.

6.   *New Catholic Encyclopedia*, p. 559.

7. Hyginus Eugene Cardinale, *The Holy See and the International Order* (Gerrards Cross, England: Colin Smythe, 1976), pp. 101, 102.

8. Cardinale, p. 102.

9. Cardinale, p. 102.

10. Cardinale, p. 115.

11. Graham, p. 30.

12. Cardinale, p. 95.

13. Graham, pp. 27-28.

14. Graham, pp. 385-396.

15. Cardinale, p. 82.

16. Cardinale, p. 83.

17. James A. Coriden, Thomas J. Green, and Donald E. Heintschel, eds., *The Code of Canon Law* (Mahwah, New Jersey: Paulist Press, 1985), pp. 294-295.

18. Coriden, Green, and Heintschel, p. 295.

19. Graham, p. 128.

20. Graham, p. 133.

21. Coriden, Green, and Heintschel, p. 295.

22. Coriden, Green and Heintschel, p. 302.

23. Graham, p. 182, footnote, author's translation.

24. Mario Oliveri, *The Representatives* (Gerrards Cross, England: Van Duren Publishers, 1980), p. 112.

25. Gino Paro, *The Right of Papal Legation* (Washington, D.C.: The Catholic University of America Press, 1947), pp. 144, 145, 188.

26. Graham, p. 395.

27. James J. Hennesey, S. J., *America*, "U.S. Representative at the Vatican," 113:708, Dec. 4, 1965.

28. Pope John XXIII, "Humanae Salutis," in Walter M. Abbott, ed., *The Documents of Vatican II* (New York: Herder and Herder, 1966), pp. 706-707.

29. Philip Schaff, *History of the Christian Church*, vol. V, *The Middle Ages* (Grand Rapids, Michigan: Wm. B. Eerdmans Publishing Company, 1957), p. 174.

30. Schaff, p. 157.

31. Pope John XXIII, in Walter M. Abbott, p. 707.

32. Oliveri, p. 116.

33. Graham, p. 82.

34. Graham, pp. 83-84.

35. Graham, p. 328.

36. B. B. Beach, statement prepared for the House Appropriations Committee of the U.S. Congress, Subcommittee on Commerce, Justice, State, the Judiciary, and Related Agencies, 9 February 1984, p. 2.

37. *Ibid.*, p. 9.

38. Thomas J. Reese, "Diplomatic Relations With the Vatican," *America*, 16 March 1985, p. 216.

39. Reese, p. 216.

40. Reese, p. 216.
41. Reese, p. 216.
42. "Religious Organizations Urge Administration Not to Name Ambassador to the Vatican," *Congressional Quarterly*, 17 December 1983, p. 2677.
43. "A Quest for Morality," *Church and State*, November 1985, p. 4.
44. Church and State, p. 5.
45. Church and State, November 1986, p. 16.
46. Church and State, p. 17.

CHAPTER FIVE

CANON LAW AND PAPAL
UNIVERSAL JURISDICTION

1.   Margaret Deanesly, *A History of the Medieval Church, 590-1500,* 8th ed. (London: Muthuen and Company, Ltd., 1954), p. 179.
2.   Hans Lietzmann, trans. Bertram Lee Woolf, *From Constantine to Julian*, vol. 3, *A History of the Early Church* (London: Lutterworth Press, 1950), p. 82.
3.   Williston Walker, *A History of the Christian Church* (New York: Chrales Scribner's Sons, 1959), p. 105.
4.   William A. Dunning, *A History of Political Theories, Ancient and Mediaeval* (New York: The Macmillan Company, 1913) p. 133.
5.   Walker, p. 105.
6.   Charles J. Hefele, *A History of the Christian Councils* (Edinburgh: T. and T. Clark, 1896), vol. 1, pp. 181-182.
7.   Hefele, pp. 355-439.
8.   Louis Duchesne, *Early History of the Christian Church*, 4th ed. (New York: Longmans, Green and Company, n.d.), vol. 2, pp. 171-181.
9.   Hefele, Vol. 2, pp. 86-172.
10. Hefele, p. 128.
11. James T. Shotwell and Louise R. Loomis, *The See of Peter* (New York: Columbia University Press, 1927), p. 672.
12. Shotwell and Loomis, p. 675.
13. Shotwell and Loomis, *p. 675.*
14. Joseph Cullen Ayer, *A Source Book for Ancient Church History* (New York: Charles Scribner's Sons, 1941), p. 354.
15. Ayer, p. 354.
16. H. Burn-Murdoch, *The Development of the Papacy* (London: Faber and Faber Limited, 1954), p. 228.
17. Philip Hughes, *A History of the Church* (New York: Sheed and Ward, 1934), vol. II, p. 55.
18. F. W. Puller, *The Primitive Saints and the See of Rome* (London: Longmans, Green and Company, 1900), p. 196.

19. Puller, p. 201.

20. Puller, p. 196.

21. Hefele, vol. 3, p. 317.

22. Hefele, vol. 3, p. 354.

23. Hefele, vol. 3, pp. 383-422.

24. Alexander C. Flick, *The Rise of the Medieval Church* (New York: Burt Franklin, 1909), p. 297.

25. Deanesly, p. 9.

26. Thomas Greenwood, *Cathedra Petri: A Political History of the Great Latin Patriarchate* (London: C. J. Stewart, 1856), book III, chap. IV, p. 135.

27. Flick, p. 179.

28. Flick, pp. 179-180.

29. Philip Schaff, *History of the Christian Church,* vol. III, *Nicene and Post-Nicene Christianity* (Grand Rapids, Michigan: Wm. B. Eerdmans Publishing Company, 1957), p. 328.

30. Philip Schaff, *History of the Christian Church,* vol. IV, *Mediaeval Christianity* (Grand Rapids, Michigan: Wm. B. Eerdmans Publishing Company, 1910), p. 212.

31. Walker, p. 173.

32. George Lewis, trans., *St. Bernard on Consideration* (Oxford: Clarendon Press, 1903), book I, chapter IV, sect. 5, p. 20.

33. See J. F. von Schulte, "Canon Law," *The New Schaff-Herzog Encyclopedia of Religious Knowledge,* vol. 2, pp. 381-388.

34. Marshall W. Baldwin, *The Medieval Papacy in Action* (New York: The Macmillan Company, 1940), p. 69.

35. L. Elliott Binns, *The History of the Decline and Fall of the Medieval Papacy* (Anchon Books, 1967), p. 4.

36. Thomas N. Parker, *Christianity and the State in the Light of History* (London: Adam and Charles Black, 1955), p. 128.

37. Binns, p. 128..

38. Baldwin, p. 69.

39. Charles Augustine, *A Commentary on the New Code of Canon Law,* vol. II, *Clergy and Hierarchy,* 5th ed. rev. (St. Louis: B. Herder Book Company, 1928), pp. 207-216.

40. H. A. Ayrinhac, *Constitution of the Church* (New York: Blase Benziger and Company, Inc., 1925), pp. 27-28.

41. Augustine, vol, I, *Introduction and General Rules* (canons 1-86), p. 10.

42. Augustine, vol. VIII, book 5, *Penal Code* (canons 2195-2414) (St. Louis: B. Herder Book Company,1924), p. 84.

43. Augustine, vol. II, pp. 224, 217.

44. James A. Coriden, Thomas J. Green, and Donald E. Heintschel, eds., *The Code of Canon Law: A Text and Commentary* (Mahwah, New Jersey: Paulist Press, 1985), pp. 266, 271.

45. Coriden, Green and Heintschel, pp. 951, 959.

46. Coriden, Green and Heintschel, p. 265.

47. Walter M. Abbott, ed., *The Documents of Vatican II* (New York: Herder and Herder, 1966), p. 38.
48. Abbott, p. 38.
49. Abbott, p. 43.
50. Abbott, p. 43.
51. Abbott, p. 44.
52. Abbott, p. 721.
53. Abbott, p. 721.
54. Abbott, pp. 721-724.

CHAPTER SIX

CATHOLICITY AND ECUMENISM

1. Jaroslav Pelikan, *The Riddle of Roman Catholicism* (New York: Abingdon Press, 1959), pp. 50, 46.
2. Edward C. Fendt, ed., *What Lutherans Are Thinking* (Columbus, Ohio: The Wartburg Press, 1947), p. 22.
3. Harold J. Grimm, *The Reformation Era* (New York: The Macmillan Company, 1954), p. 125.
4. Martin Luther, *Three Treatises* (Philadelphia: The Muhlenberg Press, 1943), pp. 12-13.
5. Luther, p. 16.
6. Luther, pp. 20-21.
7. Luther, pp. 23, 25.
8. Luther, pp. 115-245.
9. Luther, p. 249.
10. Henry Bettenson, selector and ed., *Documents of the Christian Church* (London: Oxford University Press, 1943), p. 285.
11. Pelikan, pp. 50-51.
12. John T. McNeill, *Unitive Protestantism* (Richmond, Virginia: John Knox Press, 1964), pp. 86-87.
13. "The Canons and Decrees of the Council of Trent," in Philip Schaff, *The Creeds of Christendom*, vol, II, *The Greek and Latin Creeds* (New York: Harper & Brothers, 1877), p. 113.
14. Pope Pius IV, "Profession of the Tridentine Faith," in Schaff, pp. 207, 209-210.
15. Pope Pius IX, "The Papal Syllabus of Errors," in Schaff, p. 212.
16. Pope Pius IX, pp. 219, 222, 227.
17. Geddes MacGregor, *The Vatican Revolution* (Boston: Beacon Hill, 1957), p. 35.
18. A. B. Hasler, *How the Pope Became Infallible* (Garden City, New York: Doubleday and Company, Inc., 1981), pp. 80-81.

19. Kenneth Scott Latourette, *Christianity in a Revolutionary Age,* vol. 1, *The Nineteenth Century in Europe* (New York: Harper & Brothers, 1958), p.285.

20. Henry Denzinger, trans. Roy J. Deferrari, *The Sources of Catholic Dogma* (St. Louis: B. Herder Book Company, 1957), p. 464.

21. Walther von Loewenich, trans. Reginald H. Fuller, *Modern Catholicism* (New York: St. Martin's Press, Inc., 1959), p. 266.

22. von Loewenich, p. 266.

23. *The Promotion of True Religious Unity: Encyclical Letter (Mortalium animos) of His Holiness, Pope Pius XI* (Washington, D. C.: National Catholic Welfare Conference, 1928), pp. 1-4, *passim.*

24. *The Promotion of True Religious Unity,* p. 12.

25. *The Promotion of True Religious Unity,* p. 13.

26. *The Promotion of True Religious Unity,* p. 14.

27. *The Promotion of True Religious Unity,* pp. 15-17, *passim.*

28. Harold E. Fey, ed., *The Ecumenical Advance,* vol. 2, *A History of the Ecumenical Movement, 1948-1968* (Philadelphia: The Westminster Press, 1970), pp. 316-317.

29. Denzinger, p. 648.

30. J. N. D. Kelly, *The Oxford Dictionary of Popes* (Oxford: Oxford University Press, 1986), p. 310.

31. Walter M. Abbott, ed., *The Documents of Vatican II* (New York: Herder and Herder. 1966), p. 713.

32. Abbott, p. 715.

33. Abbott, p. 354.

34. Abbott, p. 363.

35. Abbott, p. 365.

36. Austin Flannery, ed., *Vatican II on the Church* (Dublin: Scepter Books, 1967), foreword.

37. Abbott, p. 710.

38. Abbott, p. 716.

39. Abbott, p. 717.

40. Abbott, p. 387.

41. Abbott, p. 388

42. Abbott, p. 361.

43. Abbott, p. 345.

44. Abbott, pp. 369-370.

45. Abbott, p. 346.

46. Abbott, pp. 660-668.

47. Abbott, pp. 662-663.

48. Abbott, p. 219.

49. Bert Beverly Beach, *Vatican II: Bridging the Abyss* (Washington, D.C.: Review and Herald Publishing Association, 1968), p. 284.

CHAPTER SEVEN

MEDIEVAL THEORISTS AND
PAPAL UNIVERSAL SUPREMACY

1.   J. M. Parker, *Christianity and the State in the Light of History* (New York: Harper and Brothers, 1955), p. 133.
2.   A. P. D'Entreves, *The Medieval Contribution to Political Thought* (Oxford: Oxford University Press, 1939), p. 44.
3.   R. L. Poole, *Illustrations on the History of Medieval Thought and Learning* (London: Society for Promoting Christian Knowledge, 1920), p. 238.
4.   E. Emerton, "The Defensor Pacis of Marsiglio of Padua," in *Harvard Theological Studies* (Cambridge: Harvard University Press, n.d.), vol. VIII, p. 1.
5.   Marsilius of Padua, trans. Alan Gewirth, *The Defender of Peace,* vol. II: 'Defensor pacis' (New York: Columbia University Press, 1956), p. 431.
6.   Marsilius of Padua, p. 425.
7.   Marsilius of Padua, p. 7.
8.   Marsilius of Padua, p. 7.
9.   Marsilius of Padua, p. 34.
10.   Marsilius of Padua, pp. 51-53, *passim.*
11.   D'Entreves, pp. 62-63.
12.   Marsilius of Padua, p. 103.
13.   Marsilius of Padua, p. 103.
14.   Marsilius of Padua, p. 323.
15.   G. H. Sabine, *A History of Political Theory* (New York: Holt, Rinehart and Winston, Inc., 1937), pp. 300-301.
16.   Alan Gewirth, *Marsilius of Padua and Medieval Political Philosophy* (New York: Columbia University Press, 1951), vol. I, p. 262.
17.   Parker, p. 133.
18.   Marsilius of Padua, pp. 241-253, passim.
19.   Marsilius of Padua, p. 301.
20.   Marsilius of Padua, p. 23.
21.   Marsilius of Padua, p. 141.
22.   Marsilius of Padua, p. 234.
23.   Marsilius of Padua, p. 143.
24.   Marsilius of Padua, p. 146.
25.   Marsilius of Padua, p. 240.
26.   Marsilius of Padua, p. 148.
27.   Marsilius of Padua, p. 151.
28.   Marsilius of Padua, pp. 261-262.
29.   Marsilius of Padua, p. 262.
30.   Marsilius of Padua, pp. 259, 261.
31.   Marsilius of Padua, pp. 280-281.

32. Marsilius of Padua, p. 287.
33. Marsilius of Padua, p. 305.
34. Marsilius of Padua, p. 305.
35. Emerton, p. 55.
36. Gewirth, p. 9.
37. F. Sander, "Marsilius of Padua," in *The New Schaff-Herzog Encyclope-dia of Religious Knowledge,* vol. VII, p. 209.
38. Charles Augustine, *A Commentary on the New Code of Canon Law,* vol. II, *Clergy and Hierarchy* (St. Louis, Missouri: B. Herder Book Company, 1928), pp. 208-209.
39. Sander, p. 209.
40. Otto Gierke, *Political Theories of the Middle Age* (Boston: Cambridge University Press, 1900), p. 19.
41. Philip Schaff, *History of the Christian Church,* vol. V, *The Middle Ages, 1049-1294* (Grand Rapids, Michigan: Wm. B. Eerdmans Publishing Company, 1957), p. 209.
42. Thomas Aquinas, *Commentum in IV Libros Sententiarum,* in Ewart Lewis, *Medieval Political Ideas* (London: Routledge and Kegan Paul, 1954), vol. 2, p. 567.
43. Reinhold Seeberg, trans. Charles E. Hay, *Textbook of the History of Doctrines* (Grand Rapids, Michigan: Baker Book House, 1958), vol. II, p. 146.
44. A. P. D'Entreves, *Medieval Contribution to Political Thought* (Oxford: Oxford University Press, 1939), p. 19.
45. Schaff, p. 590.
46. Frederick Copleston, *A History of Philosophy* (London: Burns Oates and Washbourne, Ltd., 1953), vol. III, p. 44.
47. J. P. Mayer, *Political Thought: The European Tradition* (New York: The Viking Press, 1939), p. 102.
48. Stephen C. Tornay, *Ockham: Studies and Selections* (LaSalle, Illinois: The Open Court Publishing Company, 1938), p. 81.
49. Tornay, p. 81.
50. William of Occam, *De Imperatorum et Pontificum Potestate,* in Ewart Lewis, p. 606.
51. William of Occam, p. 607.
52. William of Occam, p. 611.
53. William of Occam, p. 606-607.
54. R. Seeberg, "Occom", *The New Schaff-Herzog Encyclopedia of Religious Knowledge,* vol. VIII, pp. 219, 220.
55. William A. Mueller, *Church and State in Luther and Calvin* (Nashville, Tennessee: Broadman Press, 1954), pp. 37-38.
56. Schaff, vol. VII, *Modern Christianity: The German Reformation,* p. 543.
57. Schaff, p. 543.
58. Karl Holl, in Mueller, p. 34.
59. J. L. Neve, in Mueller, p. 166.

60. Calvin, *Institutes*, book IV, chap. 20, par. 4, in Henry Beveridge, trans., *Institutes of the Christian Religion by John Calvin* (Grand Rapids, Michigan: Wm. B. Eerdmans Publishing Company, 1957), vol. 2, pp. 653, 654.

61. Calvin, par. 29, in Beveridge, pp. 673-674.

62. Schaff, p. 546.

63. Georgia Harkness, *John Calvin, the Man and His Ethics* (New York: Abingdon Press, 1931), p. 221.

64. Mueller, pp. 115-116.

CHAPTER EIGHT

THE DEVELOPMENT OF RELIGIOUS LIBERTY

1. William Temple, *Citizen and Churchman* (London: Eyre and Spottiswoode, 1947), p. 67.

2. G. C. Berkouwer, *Man: The Image of God* (Grand Rapids, Michigan: Wm. B. Eerdmans Publishing Company, 1962), pp. 330, 331.

3. Martin Luther, in M. Searle Bates, *Religious Liberty: An Inquiry* (New York and London: Harper & Brothers, 1945), p. 155.

4. Philip Melanchthon, in J. Warns, *Baptism* (London: The Paternoster Press, 1957), p. 178.

5. Warns, pp. 182-183.

6. Warns, p. 181.

7. Sebastian Castellio, trans. R. H. Bainton, *Concerning Heretics* (New York: Columbia University Press, 1935), p. 342, in Bates, p. 156.

8. Roland H. Bainton, *The Travail of Religious Liberty* (New York: Harper and Brothers, 1951), pp. 91, 94.

9. Philip Schaff, *The Progress of Religious Freedom* (New York: Charles Scribner's Sons, 1889), p. 16.

10. Bainton, p. 55.

11. Schaff, pp. 19-20.

12. Schaff, p. 21.

13. Schaff, p. 25.

14. Schaff, pp. 87-112.

15. Schaff, pp. 87-125.

16. Schaff, p. 38.

17. Schaff, pp. 46-47.

18. Frank M. Anderson, *Constitutions and Other Select Documents Illustrative of the History of France, 1789-1907* (Minneapolis, Minnesota: The B. W. Wilson Company, 1908), p. 172.

19. Philip Schaff, *The Creeds of Christendom*, vol. III, *Nicene and Post-Nicene Christianity* (New York: Harper and Brothers, 1877), p. 645.

20. Schaff, *The Progress of Religious Freedom*, p. 63.

21. Walter M. Abbott, ed., *The Documents of Vatican II* (New York: Herder and Herder, 1966), pp. 678-679.

22. Pope John Paul II, in *Second World Congress on Religious Liberty Proceedings* (Washington, D.C.: International Religious Liberty Association, 1984), p. 149, citing a March 10, 1984, address to the Fifth International Colloquium of Juridical Studies.

23. Raymond F. Cottrell, "The Declaration on Religious Liberty," *Review and Herald,* 142: 2-5, October 21, 1965.

24. Abbott, p. 673.

25. Abbott, p. 699.

26. *Christian Science Monitor*, September 24, 1965, in Paul Blanshard, *Paul Blanshard on Vatican II* (Boston: Beacon Press, 1966), p. 96.

27. Abbott, p. 677.

28. A. F. Carillo de Albornoz, "The Ecumenical and World Significance of the Vatican Declaration on Religious Liberty," in B. B. Beach, *Vatican II: Bridging the Abyss* (Washington, D.C.: Review and Herald Publishing Association, 1968), p. 194.

29. Abbott, p. 685.

30. Abbott, p. 685.

31. Abbott, p. 683.

32. Abbott, p. 684.

33. Abbott, p. 684.

CHAPTER NINE

THE RELIGIOUS ROOTS AND PRINCIPLES OF AMERICAN DEMOCRACY

1. Richard B. Morris, ed., *Encyclopedia of American History* (New York: Harper and Brothers, 1953), p. 33.

2. *Academic American Encyclopedia* (Danbury, Connecticut: Grolier Incorporated, 1984), vol, 6, p. 75.

3. *Academic American Encyclopedia*, vol. 5, p. 215.

4. *Academic American Encyclopedia*, p. 220.

5. Morris, p. 85.

6. Adrienne Koch and William Peden, *The Life and Selected Writings of Thomas Jefferson* (New York: Random House, 1944), p. 554.

7. Philip Schaff, *The Progress of Religious Freedom* (New York: Charles Scribner's Sons, 1889), p. 1.

8. Schaff, p. 85.

9. A. D. Lindsay, *The Modern Democratic State* (London: Oxford University Press), pp. 117-118.

10. Lindsay, p. 12.

11. Ernst Troeltsch, *The Social Teaching of the Christian Churches* (New York: Harper and Row, 1931), vol. II, p. 671.

12. Albert Hyma, *Christianity and Politics* (New York: J. B. Lippincott Company, 1938), pp. 239, 241.

13. Loren P. Beth, *The American Theory of Church and State* (Gainsville, Florida: University of Florida Press, 1958), p. 53.

14. James Hastings Nichols, *Democracy and the Churches* (Philadelphia: The Westminster Press, 1951), p. 17.

15. Nichols, pp. 39, 42, 43, 133.

16. M. Searle Bates, *Religious Liberty: An Inquiry* (New York: Harper and Brothers, 1945), p. 476.

17. Thomas Paine, *Rights of Man* (New York: Willey Book Company, 1942), pp. 33-34.

18. Robert Stewart, compiler, *A Dictionary of Political Quotations* (London: Europa Publications Limited, 1984), p. 141.

19. James F. Green, *The United Nations on Human Rights* (Washington, D.C.: The Brookings Institution, 1956), pp. 175-177.

20. B. B. Beach, in *Second World Congress on Religious Liberty Proceedings* (Washington, D.C.: International Religious Liberty Association, 1984), introduction.

21. Lewis C. Henry, *Five Thousand Quotations for All Occasions* (New York: Doubleday and Company, Inc., 1945), p. 100.

22. Henry, p. 126.

23. Nichols, p. 279.

24. Charles Augustine, *A Commentary on the New Code of Canon Law*, vol. II, *Clergy and Hierarchy* (St. Louis, Missouri: B. Herder Book Company, 1928), pp. 208-209.

25. Philip Schaff, *The Creeds of Christendom*, vol, II, *The Greek and Latin Creeds* (New York: Harper and Brothers, 1877), pp. 222, 227.

26. E. Emerton, "The Defensor Pacis of Marsiglio of Padua," *Harvard Theological Studies* (Cambridge: Harvard University Press, 1920), vol. VIII, p. 81.

27. Augustine Cardinal Bea, *The Unity of Christians* (New York: Herder and Herder, 1963), pp. 144, 176-177.

28. F. W. Farrar, *History of Interpretation* (New York: E.P. Dutton and Co., 1886), p. 331.

29. Constant H. Jacquet, ed., *Yearbook of American and Canadian Churches, 1986* (Nashville, Tennessee: Abingdon Press, 1986), pp. 246, 248, 249, 283.

30. David B. Barrett, ed., *World Christian Encyclopedia* (Oxford: Oxford University press, 1982), pp. 714, 724.

31. Barrett, p. 719.

CHAPTER TEN

POSTSCRIPT: THE ESCHATOLOGICAL DIMENSION

1. Walter M. Abbott, ed., *The Documents of Vatican II* (New York: Herder and Herder, 1966), p. 712.

INDEX